she walks for days inside a thousand eyes

she walks for days
inside a thousand eyes

a two-spirit story

Sharron Proulx-Turner

TURNSTONE PRESS

Turnstone Press
Artspace Building
018-100 Arthur Street
Winnipeg, MB
R3B 1H3 Canada
www.TurnstonePress.com

Turnstone Press gratefully acknowledges the assistance of the Canada Council for the Arts,
the Manitoba Arts Council, the Government of Canada through the Book Publishing
Industry Development Program, and the Government of Manitoba through the
Department of Culture, Heritage and Tourism, Arts Branch, for our publishing activities.

Cover design: Jamis Paulson
Cover image: Caw...Caw...Caw...*The Encounter* by Clô Laurencelle
Interior design: Sharon Caseburg
Printed and bound in Canada by Friesens for Turnstone Press.

Mixed Sources
Cert no. SW-COC-001271
© 1996 FSC

Library and Archives Canada Cataloguing in Publication

Proulx-Turner, Sharron
    She walks for days inside a thousand eyes : a two spirit story / Sharron Proulx-Turner.

Poems.
ISBN 978-0-88801-326-2

    1. Two-spirit people—Canada—Poetry. I. Title.

PS8581.R68983S54 2008   C811'.6   C2007-901884-X

to my grandmother, Germaine Marguerite Proulx-Boyce

contents

she walks for days inside a thousand eyes

as every good reporter knows: each person has
two sides

germaine:
where light beckons
without a shred of shame or blame

I've been deep inside the colours of a rainbow twice. few people have that honour. the first time I was thirty. I was in my car and, of course, drove on through. the memory of that split-second moment has always made me feel like I've been breathing sacred colour into a painting of my every-day world.

now, at fifty-four, after driving into the violet-red-yellow-two-tone-blue a second time, I'm left standing at the side of the road, my car toy-sized at my feet. ribbons suspend themselves from the clouds and lace through my fingers—same pieces I held as a newborn—their skyward motion pulling me up. as a child, I remember hearing that these very ribbons are hung for each of us by the ancients, who know we need help to move through life's challenges.

sound fluffy and surreal? what can I say? if I didn't feel so darn good inside, I'd be terrified. I stand where the ribbons land me and I wonder if these strange happenings have anything to do with the crow from my dream this morning, offering feathers to me—stunning, black feathers with intricate, colourful patterns and pictures and puzzles. the crow clings to me after giving up its feathers and I keep encouraging it to go, just fly, too cloistering. but the bird holds on, holds on, and I try to pry it off my wrists and arms. at the time I think, this is a bizarre dream with very odd boundaries. now? I'm just not so sure.

I think, maybe the ribbon-shirt I'm wearing today is somehow connected. it's so personal, a gift from the elders, the ribbons violet-red-yellow-two-tone-blue. the pride colours, being I'm a two-spirit and still learning my role. there are so many diversions along the way to keep us from our true role in life, our obligation to grow into the elders we're meant to be. I'm maturing now, and even though I sometimes feel like I'm twelve years old, I know there're people who look to me for guidance and witnessing.

I reach into my pocket and take out some tobacco to offer to ask for help from the grandmothers, from my ancestors and spirit guides, so I can pay attention and not be afraid of this place.

I put the sky-ribbon into my knapsack, and as I glance down at the ground, I see there's a small basket the colour of fire—breathtakingly beautiful—and next to that, my toy-sized car. I offer tobacco again before I put them into my knapsack and I feel less afraid as I walk in a direction where I think I see a young crow hiding behind the yellows in the trees. I begin to look for the crow, to open my heart for the secrets to this place. the answers are all inside is what goes through my head, a forest for a tree. wet dark bark and wonder leaves.

young crow:
who shakes the tree
brings new life

hey, is this a kids' story? are you hollering to me above the police sirens
and the talking traffic lights? or am I wandering around inside a pasty
finger painting made from scratch?

this is me, young crow talking from up on top of a street lamp, catching
some rays. I'm feeling dizzy after the rain, like a poem pumping
barefoot on the merry-go-round in the middle of winter. to tell you the
truth? I think of my life as a poetical trail. have ever since grade four
when I won a contest for a poem I wrote when I woke up in the middle
of the night. thought I'd cheated cuz it was so easy to write that poem.
I still remember it. a reflection of the times, it's untitled, and centred
on the page.

<pre>
                          caw
                          caw
                          caw
                          caw
        mountain is crying   crow is painting
            prairie is sighing   in a circle
        air is dying   mother's words
        willow is crying   crow is writing
            pine is sighing   in a circle
        cedar is dying   mother's words
        river is crying   crow is singing
            lake is sighing   in a circle
        ocean is dying   mother's words
        salmon is crying   crow is dancing
            dolphin is sighing   in a circle
        eagle is dying   mother's words
                          caw
                          caw
                          caw
                          caw
</pre>

now, the only reason I show up here in the first place, is I know small spotted eagle over there thinks that woman who just popped in out of the violet-red-yellow-two-tone-blue is a crow. I do too—or did—until one of my maw-caws, my mothers, tells me while I'm reciting this after-rain poem, keep your distance. wait. watch. listen. and so I do.

you see, long time ago, during the flood-time on this here turtle island? it's only crow and nokomis—grandmother—and her sacred pipe who are floating around at first. long time, too. now, as I understand it, crow flies most of the time, day and night, day and night, with nowhere to light, and from time to time nokomis says, come, crow, rest on the stem of this sacred pipe. it's after all that exercise and listening to our grandmothers and mothers that we have special gifts, us crows, and we can move around through space and time, body and spirit, like flies on wet wood.

truth is, I have a spot for this woman, soft and tender as maggots in skullbone, and I think of a way to help out when I quietly place her toy-sized car and a basket the colour of fire for her to find next to the trees. inside the basket there's a small round stone and a crow-blanket. I scribble a note and pin it to the basket, and to make myself sound old and wise, I say,

my girl,
you may fly across the great lakes
or the universe
with this crow-blanket
around you

small spotted eagle:
when time holds itself around the middle
and laughs a belly laugh

this is where it all begins
that moment   that glorious moment
violet-red-yellow-two-tone-blue
drives through a rainbow in her car
blossomed close
and blood earth red
heavy and upright
holding many trees

on the other side
there is a whisper on the wet warm ground
imagine the sound
the round water sound
inside rain

> *if you go there*
> *you'll be*
> *eternity*

after the rain, small spotted eagle, her feathers spread like butter, ready
for bannock and tea. a mountain eagle, pretending to fit in and looking
for a piece of the pie. small spotted eagle sees a fleshly woman near
the trees. at first she thinks this woman is albino crow on account
of her long silver hair and the shine on the car she's straddling, and
remembering somewhere in her something about crows and where the
food is, she hovers without hesitation, hunger leading her around like
one of those dogs she's seen on strings, happy to sniff at the edges of life.

as small spotted eagle waits for this fleshly woman to find her way,
she hears the sound of river in the distance, whose watery voice,
endangered now, sounds like downpour on cement.

water:
why people don't know what to do
when your name is spelled with water

I am water   life   I am deep   I hide myself near the
breast of mother earth   where I listen to her heartbeat
          which unites us all   all my relations   I am water and I
will not deny the power to transform emotions into knowing
          and yet   these days   each moment
seems to take my breath   my grief bleeds senseless poison pain
          oceans mountains rivers streams
life's blood of your mother   maybe because I'm feeling overrun
by excuses   underfoot   water   vital to the spirit
blood pressure   and waste   flow of emotion
               creative energy

a tiny seed   floating
in the deepest part
of her own river
like the downy glow
under a new spring leaf

face to face
to nose to cheek
shaping stories
for the skies

where moon is water's mate
whispers on the waves
that pool ahead
in the heat on the highway

dreams are the watery melodies
who touch eyes body tongue
like water
with the power to revive
people from the dead

I am water   life   a baby's love   tonight
the sky will speak   the thunderbeings

this is where the answers are
a note pinned onto a door
the only wrong answer
is the one where you are dishonest
with yourself

gopher (with one eff):
what sun is raining
inside my mother's eyes

letter to germaine:

you've been missing four weeks now
how i wish you were here
aptn asks me, do you have any comments
i shrug my shoulders
every word's a bundle
looking for a stone

i tell them, long time ago
germaine asks
what do you think of death
and i say
i think death would be exciting
i 'member you rolled with laughter
then put a green ribbon on my dream catcher
cut from around the sweetgrass above your bed

here's the eulogy interview i did about you with aptn:
for those of you who don't know me, my name is gopher (with one eff).
i'm an underearth native from turtle island. i met germaine only this
generation, just after the golf ball that took my great-grandmother's
voice. i met germaine through tragedy in my family. my great-
grandmother once told me that when you lose something, there's always
a balance, that you've also gained. often she'd say, gopher (with one
eff)? i wish you'd known me when i could talk. i had such a beautiful
voice—deep and raspy. i had a great laugh and i could really yell. i miss
being able to yell and i miss being able to sing. and me being me? i
asked, what have you gained from losing your voice, grandmother? her
answer? nothin'.

germaine laughed hard when i told her that one. germaine was real funny. she had a fine-tuned sense of humour that'll be remembered for generations to come, not to mention going to her grave without a trail off the side of the road. germaine told me, you leave a part of your light behind when it's your time to go. she said her light'll be all over the sidewalks downtown and all in the shops cuz she loved to shop. she loved to walk. she loved to read. she loved art and crocuses, sunflowers and storm clouds, and deep, deep snow.

germaine said her light'll be in her kids and grandkids for seven generations to come. be careful what you leave behind, gopher (with one eff), she said. even your thoughts go travelling, so watch what you say and think. what you say and what you do? that'll be passed down to your kids and lots of other people. today, i pass this thought around, germaine. i love you, germaine. i wish you a safe journey in the spirit world.

my love to you forever,
gopher (with one eff)

on one side, the vowel side, we find mind &
intellect, body & movement, spirit & emotion

young crow:
eh is for question mark
as in meatball soup anyone

this morning I dream I'm driving a small red car, a convertible. I live
in vancouver. I feel like the baby in the back seat and me in the driver's
seat, flying way above the road, very liberating and tasting fine. I parallel
park the car on a hill, facing up, and I go to a laundromat to pick up
my clean clothes. when I head towards the entrance I get lost in a maze
of back alleys, dimly lit with a spooky grey light. everything is washed
in this grey lifelike light, oppressive and evil, and I'm unable to find my
way to the street. yet, in all this, I'm bored. I'm a wonderland, flying
again, a bit out of control and awed by loveliness—the heat, the sun, the
greens. a lasting moment, complete and intelligent at such a young age.
sound too good to be true? well, this is me, young crow talking from this
little ribbon of highway near a flock of windmills. thought they were
scarecrows until maw-caws called me in for lunch. what can I say?

I have a story to tell, as told to me from a hospital bed. I'm in a kitchen,
sitting at the table with a woman a little older than me, bangs and
a kerchief on her head like the old ladies wear. she's talking in her
language, telling me this big long story about a crow. it's a story told
to her by her grandmother and to her by her grandmother and to her
by her grandmother, is how she says. I try to get her to speak in my
language, but she doesn't. she just talks away in her language and I'm
able to understand enough to know she's telling me about a time before,
about when the crows and the people could talk and share knowledge
verbally. this is still possible today, which is why she's telling me the
story.

the crow in the story says, better times are ahead. the woman talking
takes me outside with her and we get into a car and drive off. I'm sitting
on the passenger seat side in the back and a small spotted eagle sees me
from a ways off and starts to flag us down, but off we go, and I wave.

small spotted eagle:
ee is for after the sun goes west of the ocean
and bridges grace the land

immediately a wolf is heard howling in the east, and as small spotted
eagle looks in that direction, she sees the fleshly woman, who must be
here to learn something for her people. small spotted eagle has seen this
woman often, in the form of an ancient carving just below the surface
of the water, clear and clean and fresh water green. when the sun shines
on that work, the elegance of the violet-red-yellow-two-tone-blue is
something to behold.

this is the view from her birth site, the place where she plans to raise her
young. the carving is made from something that corrodes slowly from
the sand and the tide, the waves and the wind, and even so, time slows
there, caught in the movement.

there are scripted words, woven and broken, spiralling off into moon.
some of the words can be spoken. small spotted eagle knows these
words in a song her mother taught her, and she sings the words to life.

blooms
her woman body
skin of rain
whose blanket   glows

grows   motherthought
hands of gentle
velvet weaving
two worlds   to words

listening lifting
two-spirit's ochre face
of cloud in mirror's passing
and fire on the path

of women's hearts are drumming
                    drumming
women's hearts are drumming
                        dancing
women's hearts are dancing
        dancing
                drumming
                dancing

one day this woman will visit and she will need our help, small spotted
eagle was told. with this thought, she remembers her hunger, and the
sky fills with crows. she feels safe when the sky's filled with crows. they
look like they're going nowhere and everywhere at the same time. that's
kind of how she feels right now. there's this certain crow, a back-seat
driver, and though small spotted eagle tries to flag him down, he just
waves and motions her to follow. some other time, maybe. right now,
she'll stay here, in her home on the cliff, and witness both the fresh-
water carving and the fleshly woman's movements into the trees that
bridge the road between.

gopher (with one eff):
i've wondered what that means
love in a handbasket

letter to germaine:

i'm trying not to think of you. i'm making bracelets and necklaces
with pine needles. watching ants. climbing trees. playing kick the can.
colouring. reading. printing. drawing. running and running, walking
barefoot, polishing shoes. reading, over and over, the poem i wrote for
me and your girl, 'member? snowflake and leaf are sisters.

herman
your backyard friend
tender pulse
and quick to pull you
to his air

his touch in spring
of bitter candy
braids your hair
your arms hold hands
your branches grow

and suzie too
your frontyard pal
girlfriend
of the stars

tells her secrets
summer silk
and daylight in her arms
of lazy evening gossip
from the street

then when you're ten
those city men with hard hats

hack your friends away
your song

            frozen

this morning i dream you dancing
happy and loose-legged in the snow
arms flying you sing

prairie grasses
still summer-filled
yet rich
with ochre's touch
of leaves in wind
snow blossoms

oh, how i long for distance and time. like the distance your girl needed
after her poplar friends were killed, and i needed after my parents, my
grandparents, my sisters, my brother, my uncle and cousins were killed
by those city boys with baseball caps. 'member? they were slaughtered
in all manner of horror and me just standing there, looking, frozen with
fear. then you came along, chased them boys off, cupped your hands
around my battered self, and placed me in your basket. 'member? you
whispered gentle words into my ears, your breath warm and sweet. and
for a moment, a long and tender moment, i was without the fear.

i miss you so, germaine. i know the old ones say to let the person go, not
to grieve too much or too long, or the spirit of our loved one will not be
free to go to the other side. i pray for snow, germaine. i pray for snow.

i miss you so,
gopher (with one eff)

germaine:
oh, somebody's trying to make a joke about how long
the old people wait to get the smallest things changed

we're encouraged to blend with mother earth so we can celebrate life.
this place puts meaning to these words and I begin to feel off-kilter,
lighter somehow, and I'm undecided as to whether I should walk here,
on the land, or return to the road. it's getting late. I smell water and
realize I'm thirsty, so I walk in that direction. I'm hungry. I can't think
for the life of me why my knapsack didn't shrink, but everything inside?
my sandwiches, water bottle, diary, pencil and eraser, sketch pad. all of
them except the tobacco and the hatchet? they're all like particles
of sand.

but these are questions to be answered later. I've been sensing the
presence of people and animals, some of them here for my protection,
my guidance. I can hear the wind, holding secrets beyond anyone's
imaginings, a song, a poem come to life.

air presses against the light of this place
cottonwoods
young women showing off
redwillow labrador tea chokecherry wolfwillow
little sisters all around and reaching

and there
a grandmother cottonwood rests
still dry at her feet
lean, she says
lean on my body
and feel my strength
my love

I know I'm not dreaming, yet I'm frightened and excited, like a child in a petting zoo. childhood is when I knew my heart's for women. I was lucky. my old aunty loved women and she loved the same woman for nearly fifty years.

she told me a story, my old aunty, about a woman known as madame françois houle, a métisse who wore her sash like me, comme un homme, but she wasn't no man. you're nothing like madame françois houle, says my old aunty. that one wore deer skins and packed a knife. she worked scow, had her own crew. after hours, she could take on two pool tables, all night long, any night. made those rough, tough men furious, and their women too. one night she cleaned up two tables, and her with her lead arm broken, all plastered and wrapped. madame françois houle did other things too, like maybe she used medicine, but me? I don't believe that.

heard one time she was wild with jealous pride. see? there were rumours her lovely lover was loving someone else. when she heard this around the pool table she got so enraged she took all the little gifts—scented love notes, pressed leaves, platinum-golden two-tone ring, pool cue, undershorts—boxed them up, and buried them in ceremony with a medicine man, and he wasn't even from her own people. well, the good news is, gopher found the box down in her third chamber when she was getting ready to birth her babies. she unearthed that box with a mind to prevent those bad intentions buried there from harming mother earth and that young woman too. that gopher, she's always looking out for the two-spirits, says my old aunty. it's one of her jobs.

and what's one of mine? where am I and why do I feel like I haven't slept in days? eyes closed and I can see and I'm trying to open my eyes, violet-red-yellow-two-tone-blue.

as pronouns, once these are balanced, a person is balanced

germaine:
I thought I couldn't stay awake
some kind of bond a touch just so

rain medicine inside my body since my arrival. I open my eyes and
there's a crow, whose wings, loud and close, loud and close, so happy in
this life, life and death such close relatives. lots to say and waiting
for that moment, that most gay of moments, a joke so private and clear.

I feel disoriented and certain, my back against the grandmother
cottonwood. hunger and thirst remind me to move, and I offer tobacco
to this tree, to mother earth for these glorious moments, and, opening
my knapsack, I'm reminded about the basket the colour of fire. there's a
note pinned there, printed in a fine, delicate hand.

my girl,
you may fly across the great lakes
or the universe
with this crow-blanket
around you

immediately I smell sweetgrass. spectacular to look at, the lidded basket
is rich brown birchbark edged with intricate sweetgrass stitching. it's
small and round and fits easily in my open hand, fingers stretched to
round. on the lid there's quill work, delicate crocuses in full bloom,
surrounded by a subtle glow, violet-red-yellow-two-tone-blue.

when I remove the lid, something black pushes its way upward and out
of the box, lifelike and growing into a blanket in my hands. shaped in a
half-circle just wider than my outstretched arms, the round of it almost
touches the ground. quite literally, the blanket is woven with crow
feathers, hundreds of identical tail feathers.

tiny red stitches with an intricate pattern form the blanket's edge,
and the underside is a bright red densely woven cotton with an image
embroidered in rich black silk—an old lady sitting on what looks like a

very small island that resembles the back of a turtle. she holds a sacred pipe, and above her flies a single crow. they look alike, the old lady and the crow. around them is a night sky with a new moon and one visible star-cluster, pleiades.

the only other thing in the basket is a small round stone, no larger than the ones used to dress a water drum. when I pick up the stone, it's black and quiet and surprisingly heavy in my hand.

I'm in a daze, my movements slow, and, given everything that's happened over the past several hours, when the stone and the blanket fit easily back into the tiny basket, I know I must build a sweatlodge to prepare and purify myself inside the womb of mother earth, our true mother. when I'm reborn that way, I'll fast for four days.

first, though, I'll look for shelter and a good night's sleep, and with this thought, I see a large hollow in the grandmother tree, warm from the sun shining in from the south. the smells are wonderful, like fresh sage drying. once inside, I'm filled with content and peace. calm. leaning on the bare wood, sleepy, I can see whatever I want in the sky, even the ground, the grasses reds and yellows and greens, and the trees alive with the colours of fire. I'm filled with hope and longing, deep into my lungs and the pores of my spirit.

sitting in the doorway smoking tobacco
my spirit self is burning
a playfulness a
history of two
spirits body woman selves
violet-red-yellow-two-tone-blue

gopher (with one eff):
you'd think with all that river wound around those rocks
and moonland is through those doors

letter to germaine:

if i was still who i was for you, germaine, i'd sit with you today. you'd
remind me to live in the present, to be thankful for everything i have.
my health. my beauty. my children. my friends. i'd tell you what the
elder said yesterday when she talked about you as a person who helped
so many people and asked nothing in return, and i'd tell you of her
simple prayer for you, that you'll find your way home.

when i was little, you were my wisdom, full and sweet and constant.
you'd remind me of things lost under heavy pain, pulling like wind at
fine sand until i thought i'd burst through like a rock through glass. too
much pain. 'member? me with my eyes looking at the cracks in the sun,
the warm wood and the comfort of mother smells. my tears hot and
hollow with grief, whose face like fire, always bringing new shapes. be
still and listen for the silence inside, you'd say. listen for the love.

mostly your wisdom was silent, silent and simple, like the wind way
above the trees or the bit of sun between the leaves. the smell inside long
grass or the water, loud and quiet all at the same time. 'member?

all my love,
gopher (with one eff)

p.s. a gentle wind blows in from the south. i see you there, eye-level and
child-like.

young crow:
she hangs on to love lines
like memories from a spoon

I'm pretty sure that's small spotted eagle over there, leaning over the edge of a cliff like a hang-glider on wabbled stilts. this is me, young crow talking, and I've had just about enough wind for one day. I feel like my mouth is full of half-chewed paper, someone else's nervous verse I didn't even bother to read, but gives me something to do that shows I can't talk cuz my mouth is full.

now I'm not trying to be cheeky, I'm just trying to stay cool, cool and calm in the face of a horizontal wind on a blistery day. ever wonder where crows go in a wind like that? I know I used to until all my poetry blew straight into the river. and such poetry, too. I was learning my lovely lines by heart, you know? had them perched there on a branch, then—poof. memorized one, though. I still remember it. it was number ix in a series called, a noun is a noun is a dead bled noun.

but I'm getting off the eaten kak. it's not always about me, eh? I do have a sapped up story about the woman who's not a crow, but I'll save that one for another time. for now I'll tell you this version. maw-caws ask me to put that basket near the trees. it's after I get a good look at her from in the leaves that I remember, I actually know this fleshly woman. she's the one who led rally after rally to ensure the geese could nest on top of office buildings and apartment squares, hotels and fire stations. less harm from the city folk to the newborns.

once, after one of them rallies, I seen her sitting in her car having tea and bannock with cheez wiz and blueberry jam. she was with her sister, and I really wanted her to know I was interested in talking some time about saving the world and other old-fashioned topics of action and stardom, so I offered her one of my most beautiful tail feathers, one with a perfect circle-shape shaved off by that old far-sighted green hummingbird. I even wrote a poem about it.

so that's what I do
I let that feather go
on that sleepy wednesday
february day
slow   slow
slow as they go
spirals with the wind and the sun
the chinook and the day

and, you know? that fleshly woman got out of her car and walked the
block and a half to reach that feather in the middle of the road. stopped
traffic with her hand out like one of them school patrol kids. bent over
and picked up that feather with the letter oh, placed tobacco there and
a nice round shiny paperclip.

see? I still have that paperclip right here. it's one of them italian-style
ones, round and spiralled like the wind. saved some of my poems from
that wind too, did that paperclip.

so that's how we begin again, slow at first, and real powerful like. me
and that very same fleshly woman sleeping over there, all wound and
round, half-in, half-out of that grandmother tree.

small spotted eagle:
they came on the voice of fire
hot and hungry

there's this certain crow, a game-boy rider he calls himself. small spotted
eagle sees him tailing among the others, and before she knows it he's on
her back, painfully, holding on for his life. turns out that crow's afraid
of heights, though he only admits this in so many words. what he says
is, crow at one time was pure white, with the sweetest singing voice of
all the birds. like many others, he volunteers to steal fire from the people
who live east of grandmother moon, but, being a perfectionist, he
takes so long hovering over the fire—trying to find the perfect piece to
steal—his white feathers smoke to black. when he returns to his village
he tries to sing the first rap tune, but he'd inhaled so much smoke that
out comes a raw, caw, caw.

and his flight pattern's been off ever since. small spotted eagle opens
her mouth to speak, but that cawbird won't stop his talk, all panic and
green. small spotted eagle's been instructed to tell two stories for the
fleshly woman to know before she presents herself in ceremony and this
is why she's up here at her cliff home, to focus and to be alone with the
wind. but small spotted eagle must be patient. she has learned that crow
comes to only those few who already possess wisdom. crow is showy,
and then again, likes to speak in private, and small spotted eagle knows
whatever it is this one wants to share must be important if he's willing
to face his greatest fear to come to her like this. as he's managed to blurt
out, he's petrified of heights, and for him to come up here, fear wide
open, he knows she'll protect whatever mysteries he may share. and so
she listens and waits for her turn to tell him why she's here.

the crow tells small spotted eagle, he's sorry to zero in on her like this,
but he's just returned from europe and he lost his wallet over there
when he was in a lineup at a drive-through bank machine. lost his
game-boy-toy and lost count of his airmiles too. counting being one of
his secondary passions, these are great losses to him and he needs time
by the water to crash—and that's why he showed up here. that, and now
the fleshly woman over there.

small spotted eagle tells him she, too, is here for the fleshly woman, who's the one in the song taught by the ancients, the same fleshly woman who's carved into the water. small spotted eagle instructs the little crow to look below and listen, for she must tell the first story before the woman wakes up and enters into ceremony.

this is where it all begins
a world a wind away
whose edges
ripe with new life
a prayer an undertone
their sound familiar
and long

she'll fast for the future
from the past
a whisper
violet-red-yellow-two-tone-blue

and even now
the air   hushed
inside the flames
and the river just moments away

long time ago
seven young michahai yokuts women
who, out of respect for their parents
their grandparents
do not question, in their youth
the promise of beautiful young men
of marriage
in the good way of the time

with age, time slows, like wind on stone
after a storm, whose water washes
cleanses, softens
their delicate intent, unwinds

unable to love their husbands, as women do
seven young women
put onion in their hair, their clothes, their breath
their beds
to keep their men
away

the years pass in stillness, and still
seven young women search for a way
away

a way to escape from married life
once and for all
time

and so, seven young women pray, fast, six full days
their bones, parched and raining fire
of power like no other

it's then they know the two-spirits
are meant to be together
to be singers, seers, interpreters of dreams
mediators, healers
to see
as she
as he
to be
as he
as she

two, entwined in one
spirits female to male
spirits male to female

and after they fast six full days
seven young women make their way
to a cliff, so high above the trees
their moons go, their breath
slow

and there, on ropes of eagle down
six of the young women, go
their movements
slow

eagle down rises, to carry
six young women to the star world
to become, pleiades of taurus

and there, many hundreds of star sisters
hidden from the ordinary human eye, are protected
by six young women, who are visible
who surround the many hundreds of star sisters
for all time

in due time, seven young husbands
follow

yet even celestial, six young women
do not wish seven young husbands
near

seven young husbands
become aldebaran, red star of taurus
whose gift of brilliance, holds
forever to follow
six young women, of pleiades

one young woman, the youngest
remains with mother earth, transforms
to stone

this stone is mother
to a small round stone
held here, until the time is right

on the other side are the correlatives for a
balanced life: education, process & ceremony

small spotted eagle:
people who judge are both caught in fear
and do not know who they are

small spotted eagle is tired from holding so much weight on her back.
even though the clever crow makes like he's going to hop into her
nest to rest countless times, when small spotted eagle finishes her first
ancient story, the crow cocks his head and tells her instead, does she
know crow is the one who invented corn dogs? happened one time
after a feature film where the main character looked so much like a
scarecrow, every cob appeared in the credits. but that's the least of his
poems, he tells her. this morning his computer froze up real sudden like,
which is why he needs her help on this fine feathered day.

this in-crowd crow says he's betting a second basket might be waiting
at the side of the road for the woman. this basket is from the world of
the fleshly folk, from the woman's young gopher friend, the one that's
missing an eff? now, because the young crow hisself's been told so
many times by so many maw-caws he's not to mess with the other side
like some supercrow, he can't give the basket to the woman like he'd
planned. but, he'd already sent one of them emails marked urgent to the
gopher that's missing an eff just moments before he got caught in the
act, and he was scolded into giving his maw-caws his word he'd keep
his distance in return for breakfast in bed all next week—she'll need
the medicines for ceremony, kaks the little crow, she'll need to know to
throw down that very stone you talk about in your story. the little crow
buries his beak into his wing, pulls out a mechanical pencil and prints
into the air, letter by little black letter, what he's too embarrassed to say
out loud, that in his kakruffle to appear clever and wise the first time
around, he left out that part on the note he attached to the basket.

so small spotted eagle agrees to get the basket the gopher leaves and set it down next to the sweatlodge. she reminds the little crow she's here to tell another ancient story the woman must know before she wakes up. then small spotted eagle asks this clinging crow can he unhook himself from her back now and leave her feathers he's toe-combed from her wing so she can put them inside the basket? the fleshly woman will need those feathers for ceremony too, and after small spotted eagle's told the story, can the little crow stay and play awhile away, hey?

long time ago, two extraordinary two-spirit women
after dreams of future days, of prayer songs
of medicine ways, and loving only women
refuse marriage to any man

and after many years, while still young
the two women meet and grow
in power, in strength, in love

and while most young men respect these gifted ones
who see as true women, who see as true men
there are two young men who fancy themselves to be
alluring, appealing, charming, tempting
interesting, fascinating, attracting
captivating, beyond splendour

so that even after the elders tell them, no
let these women be
the men persist, and in time are forbidden
even to speak, to be
in their company

one fine summer day, all hush and hush
far into the woods
where the women peel and collect tree bark
while bathing themselves nearby
the men follow
as the women express their love
their passions sweet
and the men are witness to this
moment movement mystery time

while making love
one woman, the older one
transforms but half her beauty
into the needle of a pine
and that half floats on the water
to the mouth of her companion

the younger one, who swallows
and soon after becomes big with child
a green-eyed child whose name
soft-shell turtle woman
remains in song

so it is, that from the water
the two-spirit women obtain
their spirit power

germaine:
as sure as the moon is round
a rose is a rose is a red red rose

in the night, two traditional stories enter my dreamworld and as I'm
waking up I can still feel the breath of a spotted eagle, her voice a warm
chinook wind, fingers reaching out from the west coast sea.

first-light sun is raining
sweet green evening breezes
into the leaning orange sea
patches laced to grandmother moon
whose warm and tender floating
of crocheted loops and lullabies
trace a pattern
    heart
       to heart
  to mother sister
     daughter
       friend

I focus my eyes toward the sun, on the horizon now, and I offer tobacco
to the ancient ones, thankful for this new day. in these first moments,
as I'm still absorbing the two traditional two-spirit women's stories, I
see the face of my baby granddaughter, my son's small silver hairs, my
daughter's long expressive fingers and hands, the way she moves the hair
from her face in a brush stroke, a painting waiting to be put to canvas.
I see my partner, sitting with her back to a tree, raining warm meadows
of days.

I see myself, my future and my past. my present. I feel the fullness of
what I've been denied as a two-spirit woman. the love. the knowledge
of the ancestors. the two-spirit women from pleiades—those seen and
unseen—are in me now. they're as much a part of me as soft-shell turtle
woman is like my child.

rosehip and strawberry tea
holding hope like a freshwater bloom
close to the edge and very green

lying on the shore by the river
the water's up this year
women facing upstream
lift their chins
river passes over them
river presses into them
they're river
they're me

then, in a moment's breath, I'm seeing out from the underside of sand,
from inside the sand, upward, through freshwater green. the sand pulls
me under, holds me warm and cleans even the most intense of fears.
the sun and earth are my mothers, the moon my grandmother, and
I see the small spotted eagle looking down at me from her mother's
grandmother's nest, the young crow singing on her back.

small spotted eagle reaches down
takes my hands
and pulls me to a stand
her touch
the sea

and me
bewildered
to lose the way or road
to choose
a thought
a word
a shame a doubt
a whisper on the breeze

you can't go halfway on this road
and then stop there

these are my thoughts, random and yellow, as the morning sun shifts
under a bluebacked sky, and I am face to face with my personal power
as a two-spirit woman. I build a sweatlodge the way I've been taught,
gathering the grandmother and grandfather rocks and building a sacred
fire. so I prepare to begin my fast, with the miracle of purification, to
balance body, mind, heart, spirit, and love's shadows even the smallest
gesture. just as I see the small spotted eagle and the young crow circle
overhead, I feel the presence of many women and I prepare to enter
the sweatlodge.

gopher (with one eff):
neither the fire flared up into her friend the air
nor have the leaves begun to yellow

letter to germaine:

i'm happy to say i'm feeling much better today, and i have lots i want to say. first off, it's very cold outside and it snowed, even though there's still a fly in the fourth chamber and a couple of days ago a spider lowered in front of me from a thick evergreen, in the dark. I sensed her presence and there she was, eye-level. she asked me, am i an artist and she said, you are very beautiful, both inside and out and you have very intelligent eyes. it's only one person in a thousand looks as you do.

i'm feeling so much better i decide to check my email, and here i have a message marked urgent that's dated a while ago, from a professor wisecrow, senior vice president, otherworldly affairs. he asked me to leave a basket for you at the side of the road where you and your car went missing. he told me exactly where, and who knows how he knew, because no one else seems to. i couldn't take the chance that he's not some flybrained crow, so i'm going to do it just in case. i tried emailing him, but my reply just keeps kaking back to me, so i finally gave up. he says you'll need the four sacred medicines for ceremony and i'm to include a letter, to write a poem to proclaim the sacred medicines, and then i'm to pin a note to the basket that says,

my girl,
if you get tired from flying
you can throw down the stone to land on

i only hope this means something hopeful, and if nothing else, doing all this has made me feel so much better. just to be among the sage brings awe and healing. if you wear sage leaves in your shoes you'll walk goodness into your every move of your day and you can keep some in your pocket to protect you from any and all manner of negativity. sage is the woman's medicine and we can bless ourselves, cleanse ourselves with her incense. sage is the closest to my heart and sweetgrass is the closest to my spirit. sweetgrass is like an all-knowing doctor, a woman

46

of all ages with the attributes of a sacred, to be treated very special, to be treated with the gift of a seer, who witnesses our deepest fears and joys, who holds them for us to see like precious gems. cedar is from the deep—the deep places of mystery in our lives and can bring clarity to a puzzling behaviour at unexpected times. these medicines hold knowledge in its purest and uncensored form and, like tobacco, who represents all our relations, deliver thought, prayer, directly to the grandmothers and grandfathers.

sweet dreams germaine
and may your most tender parts
rest
on the back
of a buffalo
whose strength
whose wisdom
whose courage
will walk you into the blizzard
face first and to the place
that green green place
before the storm

love's tender tears,
gopher (with one eff)

young crow:
not only are they blueblack from rump to crown
but also each feather of a crow is brown

well if a title like that doesn't just spoil the whole effect. like the dream I have the other morning. I'm on a horse, tan brown and spotted, with a loose, long mane, a twin who was birthed with special knowledge. she's taking me to the airport and she says she thinks I'm the most grounded person she's ever met, that I do a lot for people and my memory is biased. the whole time there's this little bird in my pocket. well, well, says the little bird, now this is living, and off she goes to the mountains to have a new life. the dream goes on so long I stop off at the side of the road to get some cat kibbles and bottled water.

this is me, young crow talking, and the truth is, I have a thing for cat kibbles and bottled water that goes back to the nest. an acquired taste, says maw-caw. she tells me this story, maw-caw does. she tells me long time ago she sees this métis girl walking along with a young boy, a city boy. he's happy, you can tell by the way he licks his bubble gum ice cream, and he feels real safe with this girl in her ribbon shirt and cut-off jeans. down on the sidewalk, hopping, kind of scared-like, looking, crouching, limping, there's a baby crow. that girl says, my boy, I think that baby crow needs help. what do you think? the boy stops to look with the girl in her ribbon shirt, who leans down close and sits on the sidewalk, talks real low to that baby crow, says, you look hurt little baby, little friend, can you come with us for help? there's a vet just half a block away and we can take you there. with her gentle hold, she lifts the baby crow up to her warm.

in the vet's office, that vet person says to that girl in her ribbon shirt and cut-off jeans, you can't bring that bird in here, kid. that's a wild bird you've got there. we don't treat wild animals here. the girl looks at the baby bird and she says, you hear that, my child? they're calling you a wild animal and here you live in the city just like the rest of us, isn't it? we'll cover your ears so's you don't have to hear this kind of talk. the vet person tells her, we can give you a box for the bird or you can leave it here and we'll put it down. the bird won't feel anything, kid. you can come in while we do it if you prefer. the boy can come too.

we just want to know what's wrong with the little bird is all, says the girl. she seems injured and hungry and thirsty. she's small, as you can see, a baby still, and her eyes are cloudy with confusion. the vet person sighs real loud, ho-hums, ho-hums, says, take her away in this box, then, kid, and help her yourself if you think you can. she looks close to death anyway. it probably has bugs, you know. and how do you know it's a she?

the girl in her ribbon shirt stands there a few minutes, thinking, and the boy starts to cry softly, his ice cream dripping bubble gum smells on the outside of the box and onto the floor. the girl stands there a while longer and helps the boy feel better, tells him they'll take this little urban crow with them and help whatever way they know how. she asks do the vet people have a bit of cat food and water to spare, and they say, no, we're closing. take the wild bird and leave, kid. there's no telling what kinds of bugs and diseases that bird's brought into our waiting area and we have sick animals in the back. so, if you don't mind, kid? please. leave. the office.

so out they walk and the girl talks real gentle to that baby crow, real slow and sing-song-like as she walks over to a store to buy some cat kibbles, bottled water and a small travel pillow. well now—maw-caw always says that when she's winding down—well now, that young crow eats some of the little brown kibbles, drinks some bottled water and falls fast asleep in that box. wakes up couple hours later in the river, with the girl in her ribbon shirt washing him with the speed of an uphill leak, feather by feather.

turns out that baby crow was all tree-sapped, all stuck together like middle-of-the-road roadkill giblets on a crowded summer highway. would've died that day, that baby crow, says maw-caw. well now, wouldn't you know it? that baby crow was me, though I have to say I don't remember a darn thing except I'm sap-shy and I like my water bottled to this day.

maw-caw tells me it's cuz of what that girl in her ribbon shirt does for me that day in the river—the same woman over there who's building a sweatlodge? that's why I get along so good with the women, and that's why, like the women, I have the gift with the water. that one I didn't know myself until this one day I hear my relative talk about that at the indian friendship centre downtown over by the river. I'm playing the piano at the time and that's why I remember her violet-red-yellow-two-tone-blue words that day.

to avoid illogical shifts in person and number
lesbian has a capital elle

small spotted eagle:
two worlds split by cloud's believing
once tiny hands and tickle under there

the teachings say a woman's spiritual way is dependent on the kind of
power she possesses, the kind of spirit to whom she is attached and the
people to whom she belongs. she is required to follow the lead of her
spirit guides and to carry out the tasks they assign her, as the fleshly
woman is being asked to do now.

last night, after she tells the ancient two-spirit stories the woman must
hear before she begins her fast, small spotted eagle plays tic-tac-toe with
the bee-bop crow. when there's too little light for them to see the exes
and ohs, small spotted eagle goes to the road and picks up the basket
left there by the young gopher from the other side. the handle fills
small spotted eagle's mouth as she sets it down next to the door of the
sweatlodge. there's a note that's almost as large as the basket pinned to
the yellow braided handle.

my girl,
if you get tired from flying
you can throw down the stone to land on

small spotted eagle no sooner sets it down than the fleshly woman
comes out of the lodge and sees the basket. she reaches into her
knapsack for her tobacco, offering and praying before she reads the note
and laughs out loud. small spotted eagle thinks she hears the woman
speak through her laughter, her voice so much like her own she's left
uncertain. what she hears is like a song, full and airy.

the woman puts the small round stone into her pocket then, and she
puts the basket into her knapsack as she makes her way to rest in the
hollow of the cottonwood, wrapping herself in the crow blanket to
stay warm.

around about midnight, that cosmos crow appears out of the violet-red-yellow-two-tone-blue, crouches on a branch of the tree, and recites a long-distance poem from memory—a webmail rhythm so rich in image that the letters, the symbols themselves, burst into song. the songs in ceremony are like this, is what floats through that young crow's head. they are forever.

offering his wisdom to those who know, crow kaks at the fleshly woman, come, our friend, our sister, you've come through this invisible door and into where eagle flies through the rainbow. I'm glad I showed up just now, says that crow, cuz you're wearing the crow-blanket. I guess that means we're going for a ride while you sleep your way though the night tonight.

young crow begins to feel a joy without restraint, and small spotted eagle thinks she hears him kak-kaking something about birds flying in and out of his pockets, his hat, birds who are his life and who understand that great losses are only retrieved while flying. and as if feeling this feeling, the tree begins to shake.

the fleshly woman rises then, the crow blanket all around her. she, the grandmother cottonwood and the young crow take flight, seeing far ahead through mountains and stars and into the yellows of the night.

and now it's morning, the first morning of the fleshly woman's fast. small spotted eagle sits alone, resting on the opposite side of the cliff bank, the side her ancestors call rainbow's edge. the water below, clear and clean and fresh water green, gleams a violet-red-yellow-two-tone-blue from the early morning sun, and the underwater carving comes to life around her. she'll wait here for the crow and the fleshly woman. she knows they're inside the rock, inside the wall of the mountain she can see from where she sits. from here, too, she hears the sound of wind in the distance, whose air-sweet self is endangered now, love's tendrils slender, blood and bone.

air:
eyes swirling inside wood sounds
like the side-birds of bother

I am air   the ancients' way with words   I know
what we all do and how we go about doing it   since time
immemorial   pure and generous   I am the cool and
the wet   certainty of the ages   pay attention   the land inside
each breath   so much calm   and not nearly
enough time in one life to undo the damage that's been done

                              wind
                     blesses mother earth
                      with the warmth
                     to bear abundant life
                     the sounds you hear
                           on wind
                       are the voices
                      of the ancestors
                       who teach you
                          to sing
                     to make the music
                   given by the bird nations
                   the songs of your people
                      will never be lost
                     as long as you sit
                        and listen
                          to wind

                       when you need
                      a medicine song
                      you only have to
                       offer tobacco
                        and listen

                    soon
                    wind
                 will whisper
              the song you need
                 for healing
                 for helping
                 the people

I am air   breath of the grandfathers and grandmothers   to know
        me   is to know   storms that cut   the raw power of
lightning
          to see   to hear   in a wholly different way

                          solitude and fasting   subdue
to sing   to flee   to drum   to be   and lonely for that land
eight days   peoples of the earth   your shared prayer and song
is all that's needed to clean the air   a note pinned onto a door
                      the greatest wisdom
                          doesn't know itself

germaine:
hooked mouth to tail of flowers
yellow's winter in a full spring sun

I dream a grandmother spider comes in from the northwest, swoops
toward the southeast and through a door, forming herself into a circle,
violet-red-yellow-two-tone-blue. in that circle, a dream unwinds itself
around me as I sleep after the sweatlodge. I remember the dreams but
not much of anything else about that first night, except that I'm startled
from sleep by a rambunctious crow and somehow, someway, I've landed
in a hole or a cave or something. the space is small, and smells of wet
black leaves and cornmeal. the crow flaps around my head my arms my
eyes, which is no small miracle considering the size of the space we're in.
the crow—from the eagle's nest yesterday, I can tell by the shape of the
mouth and some of the tail feathers with perfect circle-shapes shaved
off—looks familiar, like a childhood friend.

it occurs to me I may be dead, though I feel very much alive and my
knee is bleeding from some fall I can't remember. all I can think of is I
want to hold onto the dreams and here I am stuck in a very small space
with a very panicky crow. I sit up and start to sing a quiet song out loud,
cooing in a soothing way until the crow settles into the rhythm of my
voice and lands beside my injured knee.

just when I think my knee is going to be breakfast, the crow hops onto
my left shoulder and settles there, half in, half out of my field of vision.
I tell the crow, I'm happy you're here, if even for a moment, because
you've taken my mind off my fear. before I do anything else, I need to
take the time to talk out a four-fold dream from my sleep while it's still
fresh and I would be honoured if you'd stay awhile and listen. my left
eye meets the right eye of the crow, who koo-kaks approval into my hair
my ear my spine, breath like summer. and so it is I begin to remember
my dream.

I'm sitting on the right-hand side of a couch waiting for an appointment with a doctor. there's a briefcase lying flat on the floor underneath a glass-topped table near me, and on top of the briefcase, also lying flat, is a small leather bag. it's in the shape of a suitcase but it's small, about eight inches across. it's a golden tan colour with intricate embroidery or beads or painting around the edges. I lean over to get a closer look at the smaller bag and I feel a kind of physical feeling of its beauty, of the love in the hands that crafted it.

then I begin to see pictures forming in the air above the bag. the pictures are three-dimensional, each one forming very slowly into focus and showing itself before changing its shape into the next. four pictures it shows, each in golden brown diaphanous light, like particles of sand.

picture one is mirrored in
and there, shirley bear, maliseet woman
elder, poet, artist
mimi to so many
her tiny frame
her honeybrown skin
her long silver hair
hers a redness
that would embarrass anyone
unprepared for so much voice

reaches out her hands
takes mine in hers
and recites the eastward path
her poem from *virgin bones:*
belayak kcikug'nas'ikn'ug
"the vocation of storytelling"

the winds from the east
who deliver yellow rays
which emanate
from the great warrior sun
her yellow hair
streaming
toward her sister
the earth
as she travels across the sky
what is the story that she tells us
what do the daughters say who live in the east
let us listen with our hearts
and minds
as the daughter from the east
tells her story

and she is born
she will travel on the first day to the first mountain
and she will see her skin slowly become withered
and fall off her bones
her earth skin
and skin which was so full of energies
both negative
and positive
skin's energies of indecision
boldness
hesitancy and
arrogance
a skin touched by foolishness and pride
intelligence
and wisdom
wisdom
no it is death
her elders had spoken of this little death

picture two is blended from the past
where pine scent hovers above a girl
fingers stretched and certain
reaches up and into wind
shakes loose her bark
at her base

when she dances, pine leads
marks her spirit's depth
waves branches air to river
flows glowing out to where
river reads to blanket
weaves to memories of dusk

revives to life pine leaf
a'aninin woman from the past
who speaks to me in a voice
so much like mountain water in early spring
a rainbow moves behind her
violet-red-yellow-two-tone-blue

lights up her face
her eyes mirror mine as she begins to say
I'm called barcheeampe, pine leaf
I'm adopted into the absaroke nation
I'm going to tell a humorous story here
and on another day, I'll tell more of my life

two thousand moons
have moved among us and still I'm remembered
as one of the bravest women who's ever lived
I'm known for my balance of female and male
for my intellect and grace, my strength, my courage
and my humour, even as a child
some say I'm faster than an antelope
others say a cat, clever and quiet in the trees

I was born a twin
my brother, my life, was killed in a raid on our village
hand in hand we ran from gunshots, our dog on our heels
and somehow we tripped, tumbled, tripped
and my brother hit his head, his neck broken from the fall

I was witness to his spirit's flight
became lost in my grief
felt such hate after that day
I grew to hate even my self, my life, to feel lost
inside a sadness as unyielding as fire

grief pulled at my feet
like soft yellow clay
and I prayed to the ancestors
to help me let my brother go
to our relatives in the spirit world

when I finally let him go
I have a dream where I'm an old woman
who's led many war parties
there I meet my twin, an old man
who tells me I'm to learn to fill and use
the white man's gun

to handle our indian weapons with wisdom and skill
to develop hard fine muscle
to prepare for the long life and good health
of a woman who leads men in battle

I follow the teachings of this dream
into my adult years
and though it's widely known
I love a woman who shares my home, my bed
still I'm faced with constant chirpings
from certain men

one of them, a sweet man, a brave man
a man whose stories
fill us with the sounds of our own laughter
that stays inside each of us during long battle days

day after day after year after year
asks me to marry him
he watches me like a lover
cooks for me and feeds my men
asks me to marry over and over and I tell him, no

I'm not the kind to marry any man
yet still he persists, insists I don't resist
and after many years, I tell him
well okay then, I'll marry you

I'm sure it's next morning
we'd been away from home for days
and on this morning, all bathed and shiny
his horse all shiny too
he comes to me and asks, when will you marry me then
will you marry me when we return
to the village

I laugh and laugh, I tell him, no
I'll marry you when the pine leaves
turn yellow

picture three is the colour of
buffalo bean, inside dream
and there, co'pak, klamath woman
from the past
whose undertone's a storm

and she, like eagle in her nest
her voice the wind
she tells me in future times
as in the past
a woman is what nature
or her dreams
make her
speaking only from her heart
between awake

and sleeping
where earlier than thought
is song
tracing lifetimes
distance measured
rhyme by rhyme

her voice is like the petal of a rose
smooth and serious
she tells me, even as an old woman
she's slender and agile
yet she refers to herself as a man, she says
for a man is who I am

my voice, my talk, my walk, my work, my play
all are like a man's
I'm a healer since my change of life
after being visited in dreams by the grandmothers
who pass on their teachings
who lead me into fast and ceremony
with certain medicine women of my time
for a woman is who I am

I have a love of many years
her image to this day, a tender tongue right there
more wisdom, right there behind, below her ear
more kindness, more desire
my own breath, my red sky woman
and hers were prairie skies
open between the trees
red sky woman is called to the spirit world
while we're still young
and me, I wear a bark belt
as a man does who grieves his wife
in our time
for a man is who I am

in my later years, I'm known as cherokee rose
for I was born that same tragic winter
when the cherokee were forced, barefoot
elders, infants, children, women, men
from thier homelands to okalahoma
after the indian removal act
the pain, the horror, the grief
four thousand died that winter
on that trail where they cried

after that winter, where every mother's tear fell
new flowers grew
their blossoms named cherokee rose
white pedals, for the mothers' tears
gold centre, for the gold stolen from ancestral lands
seven leaves on each stem, for the seven clans
brutally forced to leave their home
for this name I am a woman blessed
for a woman is who I am

picture four speaks
of what it is to wake up there, inside the sand
in the middle of the sun
deep within the heart
of a woman

picture four is now
a moment's glow
how two-spirit women know
their bodies' water will flow
from the shape of their ancestors

and who appears is thanadelthur
dene suline two-spirit woman
steps out from the pages of the hudson bay books
the letters lifting to the air
forming patterns along the lines
of her face, her hair, her voice
violet-red-yellow-two-tone-blue

I'm known only as slave woman in the hudson bay books
is how she begins
I'm in the spirit world a good fifty years
before pontiac's visionary decision
to drive out the british
who deliberately infested hudson's bay blankets
with smallpox
then presented them as gifts to the people
killing untold thousands of iroquois
in a matter of a few short weeks

like pontiac after me, and many since
I have a vision after a long illness
and despite the fact that I never fully recover
I'm led to translate and persuade, to mediate for peace
in the face of the limits of the english language
which seeks to split apart the mundane from the mysteries
by arbitrary means
and by this fearful rejection of knowledge
fundamental to survival, I'm at a loss
to even begin to be able to speak the spiritual bond
between the dene suline and our language

during my illness I'm taken captive by a band of cree
I'm in recovery and weak and I know there's a reason
they take me to a british post called york factory
on the western shore of what the english now call hudson bay
there I seek counsel with their leader
I know this man only as governor
I'm fluent in the english language, which seeks
many fearful splits, designed to make rigid
a perceived means of power over others
coded right into the words
whose teachings are reflected in their style
of village, of home, of walk, of talk
of manner of dress

for as long as my grandmothers remember
until the arrival of the white man
and his endless need for hides
we enjoyed a peaceful bond with the cree
now, we seek to renew that bond, and like the cree
we wish to benefit from the fur trade

I explain all this to the governor
by way of telling him how we dene suline people
like the wolf, live in clans and together we follow the caribou
in times of need we're often led to the caribou by the wolf
for wolf is not an ordinary animal
but rather enjoys spiritual gifts beyond human understanding
and because of our intimate relationship and respect for wolf
my people are lucky and will provide many furs

and so it is the governor explains to me
he may be an english but has great respect
for our ways, he says he understands
there's powerful medicine in my name
that he's heard how those with my name, like wolf
are able to travel great distances
to help their people in extraordinary ways

he tells me he once knew an anishinaubae man
who saved his life against all odds
not once, but twice
a man who shared his people's version
of the creation of this world
where wolf is teacher to the people
and in the story, wolf names
plants, trees, animals
puts words to the nature of our earth mother

later on, the great mystery
teaches both the wolf and the people
they're to walk separate paths, and when they do cross paths
to do so with respect, to remember the role of the wolf
in their beginnings

with the arrival of summer, I'm asked to mediate
to travel with the assistant to the governor
together with a band of one hundred fifty cree men
to find the dene suline traders, and escort them to york factory

travel to the west, difficult at best
with so many rivers to cross
lakes and swamps to avoid and trek around
is worsened tenfold by the weather, cold and wet
people become sick, prompting the assistant to the governor
to split the party in half

the group with the assistant to the governor
after eight days without food
meets up with me and my well-fed crew
at the site of a recent battle
where dene suline men, on their way to trade
were intercepted and killed by the cree
their furs taken and their bodies left to the wolves

the assistant to the governor and the cree men
fearful now to go on, agree to wait ten days
for my return, and on the tenth day
as the crees prepare to leave
I make my way back to camp
with enough dene suline men to do battle
or to trade

two days and nights I listen and speak
interpreting and persuading, cajoling and coaxing
enticing and flattering, until my voice is raw and hoarse
our efforts are met with happy success
for my people host a feast of friendship and peace

after our return to york factory
the governor requests my continued employment
and visits are arranged
to extend the peace, to establish trading posts
with the dene suline and other nations
along what the english call the churchill river
in this way the fur trade moves swiftly west and north
and with this movement grandmother wolf calls me home
carries me inside her mouth like a tiny babe
to the spirit world

each of these four pictures reveals itself in dreamtime—slowly,
rhythmically, like a song inside the sand—and as the fourth image
fades, I'm left still straining to see the detail beaded or embroidered
or painted on the smaller bag and I'm brought back to my senses. I
look up just long enough to see the women I've been introduced to so
far—thanadelthur, co'pak, red sky woman, barcheeampe and shirley
bear, the seven young yokuts women, soft-shell turtle woman and her
mothers, and mothers to us all, water and air—form a circle around me.
they begin to sing, to remind me to listen and remember that this, the
first day of my fast, I'm here to watch and to listen. to learn. to pray and
to sing. to still myself with this song.

ancient mother, I hear you calling
ancient mother, I hear your song
ancient mother, I feel your laughter
ancient mother, I taste your tears

young crow:
looking for a rat race and mr bean's okay
or is that lay as in neighbour or weigh

I dream I'm a flock of small birds
content with the vastness of the space
and the abundance of food
gleeful with anticipation
and we know
all we have to do is keep me upright
dress me up and send me out there
alone
ready to gather
for the spring

where, oh where did my little bird go? oh, where, oh where can he be?
this is me, young crow talking, and I just can't get that song out of my
head. reminds me of small birds, barely out of their eggs, tiny and quiet,
mouths open so wide all their secrets can be seen. maw-caws say the
tiny birds hold all the wisdom of the centuries, the intelligence of days
protected from the rain. small birds in flight? their promise is a whole
world of deep joy.

so this is my frame of mind after a bit of a brat-nap, philosophical and
kind. this is rare for me, it's true, but I wake up in a good mood after
coming down from all that cliff-clinging crapping and kaking. that's the
kind of stress no bird should have to endure, facing a fear of heights like
that. but I'd dreamed the fleshly woman fell apart all over the road like
autumn leaves, yellow and fresh and blowing in a fine, steady wind—a
wind like family ought to be—and I knew I had to follow through.
besides, I'm working on my fears, you know? maybe next is my fear
of death, eh? just the thought of death—my death that is—makes my
dainty little feet ache. oh, the horror. the horror.

that thought tuned out, all I knew was I had to go way up there to
impossible heights and talk to that small spotted eagle about my
dilemma. somehow, someway, that fleshly woman had to know about

what to do with the small round stone. and besides, now we're friends, me and that small spotted eagle, so roadkill and field fodder trade'll be a whole kak of a lot easier.

but now? how's my frame of mind now? waking up stuck here in this birdcage cave? now that's a whole other story, and all I can think about is, which shoes should I wear? that's ultimately what it comes down to, don't you think? to the I the me of me? I thought I'd be okay, you know? but there's this slo-mo moment in time in my mind where there's this guy, this big brute of a man, who keeps a tiny songbird in a cage. the bird—being a bird—sings a lot when spring's coming, right?

well, the guy? I seen him through his basement suite window. he shakes that cage so's the bird's all over the place, and yells at the top of his lungs for that bird to just shut-up! shut-up! he yells, over and over, and no sooner does he stop the shaking than the bird's right back at it, just being a songbird. tried to free that bird that day, but windows and doors kept getting in the way. that kind of treatment makes my eyes twitch, makes me think maybe alfred had the right idea after all. gives me nightmares.

just when I can no longer think, when the space in that cave becomes so small I can't breathe, can't think, can't, can't, can't, there's some little person, a paper bird, that's hanging about, singing, in the bottom right-hand corner of my field of vision. she says to me I have an open mind and an open heart and that I'm kind. I do a lot for people and I have many nice pictures on my walls. it's then that I remember where I am and I place myself on the floor long enough to realize there is a way out. there's a hole in the floor of this rock that's plenty big for ten of me. I count to ten like maw-caws tell us to do when we're all panic and green.

piyak crow sorrow
niso crows joy
nisto crows a girl
newo crows a game boy
niyanan crows silver
nikotwasik crows gold
tipakohp crows a secret never to be told
ayenanew crows a wish
kika mitataht crows a kiss
mitataht crows a time of joyous bliss

counting in michif always calms my quills. I unruffle enough to
remember that I'm with the fleshly woman and it's her that's been
singing all along. I look out the hole in the floor of the cave. at that
angle, I can see choices. they aren't any different, but they'll change the
direction of the movie, so I stay like the woman asks. I stay and while
away a fear a day as the fleshly woman talks out a long four-fold dream,
my ear on her breath like sun, love's tendrils slender, blood and bone.
then just before me and the fleshly woman are ready to make our way
through the hole, a woman appears in the opening, her skin honey-
brown, her touch, feathering into view. hands hot and alive with voice,
she tells a story so song, so sweet, of fine-spun blues to yellow.

my name is lozen, little sister, chiricahua apache woman
I was born at apacheria during troubled times
I'm here to tell you, among other things, about my beautiful love
dahteste, mescalero apache woman

how both of us, together with countless others
were forced to go into hiding for many years, to fight
to keep our people from being slaughtered
by the new people to this land, who behaved like mad, starving dogs

we're told one of our roles as women who love women
is to act as go-betweens, to help disputing groups communicate
we're best described as wealthy, as certainly I was
to have shared my love with dahteste
even to my last days, I felt her touch through a warm coat or blanket
deep as the top of a mountain, lingering and close

if I don't share my thoughts of dahteste now
I may just close a hole in the sky and let these words, their letters
blow into one another like flying ants
a swarm of queens drifting to a new place
digging themselves deep inside the mother
too busy to remember light or flight

dahteste and I met as mature women
she had children, yet after a mid-life dream
she chose the warrior's path
rode with geronimo as one of his most valued warriors and advisors

by choice, I birthed no children of my own
during my puberty ceremony, I was given the power to heal wounds
the power to find the enemy
by standing away from noise and clutter
my arms outstretched, I sang the power song I was given

singing this prayer song, while I slowly turned
any nearby enemy would cause my hands to tingle
by the sensations in my arms, I was able to say, with exact accuracy
who and where the enemy was, how many were among them

and so it was after my puberty ceremony
I was trained in battle by my older brother, victorio
himself a renowned warm springs chief
from then on I went to battle in countless campaigns
as many as any of the great apache leaders, among them cochise
juh chihuaua and victorio, mangas, coloradas and geronimo
against the mexicans and the americans

and here I'm not trying to say I was in some way
better than others, for I was an ordinary person
asked to accept extraordinary responsibilities
a reflection of the grave nature of the times
such times that I began to face mexican scalp hunters and soldiers
while I was still a girl
then in my teens, the men who call themselves americans
came in the thousands to lay claim to our homeland

forced us to be herded
like their cattle
onto square, fenced-off islands
of dry, parched land

as the years passed, my work with victorio became more pressing
for these americans who appropriated our homelands
in the black mountains, tried to confine our people
first to arizona's san carlos reservation
then new mexico's mescalero apache reservation

throughout the years, while on the battlefield
I also fulfilled my role doctoring the people
and late in victorio's campaign, I left the band
to escort a new mother with her newborn child
through mexican and american cavalry forces
across the chihuahuan desert from mexico
to the mescalero apache reservation
equipped with only a rifle and a cartridge belt
a knife and a three-day supply of food

concerned a gunshot may betray us
I used my knife to kill a longhorn for our food
then later took a mexican cavalry horse for the new mother
and escaped through a volley of gunfire

I took a vaquero's horse for myself
disappearing before he could even give chase
taking with me, along with the soldier's saddle
his rifle, ammunition, blanket and canteen
even his shirt

after I led the woman and her infant safely to the reservation
I learned that mexican and tarahumara indian forces
under commander joaquin terrazas, had ambushed
victorio and his band
at tres castillos, three stony hills, in northeastern chihuahua

terrazas surprised victorio's band in the boulders
where the warriors fought their last, and victorio fell on his own knife
rather than die at the hands of the mexicans

almost all the warriors at tres castillos were killed
many women, too, died while they fought, and of those who remained
the mexicans shot all the older people, leaving one hundred
young women and children to take to mexico for slaves

I knew the survivors would need me
so I rode alone, southwest across the desert
through american and mexican military patrols
and in the sierra madre of northwestern chihuahua
I met up with our decimated band, now led by our elder, nana

I fought beside nana and his handful of warriors
in a two-month campaign across southwestern new mexico
then, one crucial time, while I performed my duties as midwife
for a mescalero woman in childbirth
unable to perform my usual rituals prior to battle
the warriors met with tragedy

this is when I travelled across the land
to join those left strong among geronimo
and in all the terror of our time, I couldn't have known
I would feel such exquisite delight
when I arrived, where I was instructed
to meet a trusted scout and messenger

I was asked to unite with this woman, dahteste
to help her mediate between our people and the white man's cavalry
and to this day dahteste's name rings like mist in spring
no matter where I am or how I've been

I remember the very moment we met
the angle of the sun and the odours on the wind
I remember my shock and surprise, for being fluent in english
dahteste called to me, and to test my skills in the english language
she said in a tender, even tone, who could have guessed
a woman as beautiful as you would come my way today

a flush so complete took hold of me, as we both laughed long and loud
and there wasn't a moment between then and my passing
that I didn't think of dahteste with deep love and joy
as my companion for this life, and the next

even now, eyes closed, I feel our joy, our embrace,
everywhere I am
our passion, our deep love
I feel her kiss, her soft lips on my mouth, my neck, my belly
her smell, rich with hope for what's to come
and even now, though we're together in the spirit world
these wonders follow me still

unlike me, it was well known
that dahteste's beauty was matched by few women
that she took great pride in her appearance
yet like me, dahteste out-shot, out-rode, out-hunted, out-ran
almost any woman or man, with skill and grace
she was well-known for her courage, her daring and her skill
and side by side we fought in countless battles

side by side, too, we were known for our role
in the final surrender of our dear geronimo, for our efforts
to mediate day after day, for weeks and months on end,
and in the end we were deceived by the white man—rather
than our return, as promised
to the confinement of the reservations and permanent internment

we were all bound in chains and herded once again
this time as what they called prisoners of war
and from there we were put behind bars, for life

dahteste, as strong in her personal spirit
as in her warrior spirit, doctored many during prison outbreaks
of turberculosis and pneumonia
both of which killed untold millions of our people, yet she survived

after our confinement at mount vernon barracks in alabama
where I took my leave to the spirit world
after succumbing to a white man's disease
dahteste spent eight years in a florida prison
then nineteen years at the military prison at fort sill
it was only after twenty-seven years behind bars
that dahteste was finally permitted
only when she reached a very old age
to return to her people

gopher (with one eff):
soft melodies of tumbleweed
on smooth blown grass

letter to germaine:

i dream i see you flying around, higher than the sky, feeling for your
reading glasses, and words lose themselves somewhere between my
heart and my hand, inexpressible. why is it so easy to let go of one
person and so difficult to let go of another? i know it's hard to be with
someone who's stuck, no matter what the reason, even grief. staying on
in one place is hard at the best of times. life moves. days move.

still, there it is again
the silence
shhhhh
like in the trees

my strengths are hiding
inside frying pans and cake dishes
and pan-fried eggs
behind the bananas and the peanut butter
and the stawberry-rhubarb pie

a northwest winter wind
an eye eater
eating eyes

the other morning i had a dream just before i woke up. i was floating
in water, beautiful fresh water, clear with a rareness that only comes
in dreams. i felt really happy, content, and i was talking out loud,
saying something like, this is the most beautiful day of my life. i feel so
complete, i said, so good, and i'd like to keep this feeling and remember
this feeling for all eternity.

i said thank you to the grandmothers and grandfathers, to the water spirit, and i felt an incredible peace and joy deep in my body. i was floating on my back and pushing myself off rock at the edge where i'd float, rock that felt alive and vibrant.

there was a woman who looked like you, going out into the water to swim or sail or something and i said out loud, if i were a different person, that would be the most wonderful thing, to be a water person like that. but me? i'm a land person. the sky was blue and clear and the sun was hot and healing like only direct sun can be. i felt like i've rarely felt in my life.

then as i was floating and remembering how wonderful i felt, my back feet stopped me quite abruptly, hitting rock just under the surface of the water. i moved to tread water to see what was there, and here there was a carving, under the water. the water was clear and sharp with life.

the carving was rounded like any beach stone, smooth on the feet. clean. everything was stone. even the ground the stones protruded from was stone so that it was as if the stone had been carved both into and under the water. the carving looked a lot like you. i wish i knew what the dream means. i miss you so.

love in a handbasket,
gopher (with one eff)

p.s. today is the day it finally snows.
p.p.s. I hope you got my note.

to use a colon as an ochre light or arrow
faces feeling forming stories in their eyes

germaine:
a moose at the top of a mountain
and even barefoot the moon is quiet

I can't express how hard it is for me to throw down that stone and then
just free-fall from the hole in the floor of this cave. even after spending
so many hours in flight inside the warmth of that crow blanket—even
knowing what I now know from my travels toward sun, who embraces
mother earth each dawn, illuminating our life's path. I don't do heights
well and it takes me all day just to gather my courage. I spend most
of my day in prayer. I sing the prayer songs I know and I hear many
women singing these sacred songs with me.

the grandmothers are behind me, beside me and around me, singing
and speaking in many languages. I can feel them—their power and their
love—and I'm able to understand them.

one of them tells me her name is kuilix, the red one, and she transports
me to a place of windows and doors. she returns me to the inside of this
mountain only after sharing this great mystery and after introducing
three two-spirit women—her partner, pit river woman—and two other
women from the past, suya'ki and pitamakan, also partners.

my name is kuilix, kalispel woman of another time
the red one I'm called, on account of I'm so often seen
wearing a red ribbon shirt
lovingly made for me by pit river woman

when we meet those from another time
we are sister spirits, pit river woman said
sharing a moment together during dream time
during a sacred vision
learning from one another

some of us are fortunate to live out our later lives
with our love
fame is an ochre bee, pit river woman says
the day she appears before me, announcing she'll be with me
till the day we die
pit river woman told me she'd dreamed
she'd live with me after she had children

in my day, I'm known as a brave warrior who leads battles
and I'm envied for my good fortune in lasting love
but what's little known about me is my passion
for creating artwork the colour of ochre
from deep inside the mother
I work outdoors where there are windows and doors
not square but in the round, in each of the four directions
where I place my work to look at and assess

there in that place of mystery
where all four directions host a door
I can stand west and face east
and as if in dream I can see myself
standing east and facing north
or standing south and facing west

new beginnings, wisdom, time
there's where I'm both freed from the past
and I'm able to express or glimpse the future
the past, as in past my past, and beyond my own future
mathematics, poetry, song

years before pit river woman and the children
come into my life, a grandmother visits me many times
she tells me I must learn to laugh
from my inside out, at myself and in this life
such a seemingly simple request
yet for me I was quiet and serious and slow to laugh

but as time passed, even I learned to laugh
and now I'm being taught many things about the colour of blood
the colour of pipe stone, of ochre
which is said to come from the centre, the very belly
of our earth mother

each ochre drawing comes to me first in dream
in the spring and in the fall, and as each of the drawings
is completed on cloth, I hang them in the round, and wait
soon women appear in the doorways

this is why I've brought you here, germaine
to listen and to laugh
to remember these two beautiful two-spirit women
suya'ki and pitamakan, piikani blackfoot women
listen, as suya'ki tells their story
from this doorway in the round

/

I am suya'ki
piikani blackfoot woman, from a time long passed
I'm known as the friend of pitamakan, running eagle
some who tell our story after the white man's religion
out of shame, say we aren't lovers, which kills the beauty of our bond
truth is, our love is sacred, our passions deep

in our day, around our camps
I'm a widowed wife who comes to pitamakan's tipi
to do the woman's work
only I know how my softness, my gentle ways
appeal to pitamakan, even when we're still young girls

pitamakan's childhood name is brown weasel woman
when we're ten she tells me, suya'ki
I feel like I'm a boy caught inside the body of a girl
and I tell her, brown weasel woman, talk to your parents
they're known for their kindness and wisdom
they'll do the right thing

and so it is that summer brown weasel woman
begins to dress as a boy would dress, to excel in men's work
about the same time we first fall in love, for life
even though when I mature I marry a man
as arranged by my family

before she reaches her teenage years
brown weasel woman earns the nickname boy-girl
and I'm called girl-boy
not because I do the work of a boy
but because I'm known for my skills in boy play
and for my aim with a bow

one summer night as we walk in the coulees
we're young women by now and I'm big with child
brown weasel woman tells me, suya'ki
her voice so quiet, suya'ki
her voice so calm, so gentle I'm moved to tears
suya'ki, near you
my heartbeat in my ears, a breath, a dance
a lifetime sounds a longing, a song
just loud enough to blur the spaces
between my body and your words

and there we stop and touch, so tender
and I tell her, brown weasel woman
such a beautiful, simple, strong
gentle-desiring spirit you have
and that's what pulls me to you
your laugh, your wit, your grace
the way you love my body me
the way we're so happy
a happy that's easy
first kiss and my, oh my

she holds me close, her warmth
right through my belly to the child
she tells me, one day we'll live together
I know, I tell her
her voice tender, suya'ki, near you my heart
pulls blood to my throat
a song so sweet

soon after the birth of my child
my husband dies a warrior's death
and I'm free to live with my love, my life
in harmony

over twenty years I fashion pitamakan's battle clothing
loin cloth and leggings designed for comfort
beneath her woman dress
and though she leads countless expeditions, she is never proud
earns the respect of many far and wide
and like any man in her place, she holds feasts and dances
where the greatest warriors come with pride

our lodge becomes a resting place
for many women and girls
for I am taught in the ways of medicines and plants
and I, suya'ki, as are my gifts
I'm visited by married women young and old
who come for help with their troubles
and to open the mysteries of their dreams

our tenth year together
on an early winter's day
pitamakan leads a party of thirty men
to the south, where she sights and kills three buffalo
her skill is such that she does this on her own
and the following day while preparing to return home
pitamakan mounts her roan, looks to the horizon
and sees what appears to be a mist
a trick to the unwary eye

in that instant, pitamakan's powerful voice
resounds her sacred war song
as she alerts her party, then leads them into battle
against the nimi'ipuu, who wait to take them unawares

upon her return, we stretch and scrape the hides
pitamakan, the children and I
then tan them to a rare, downy texture
the two smaller robes we keep for our lodge, and on the third
a large female whose deep brown hair appeals to me
I begin to paint pitamakan's story robe
seven images I will paint
with the browns and reds and yellows of our love

I begin when the two of us are still young
and our grandparents are very old
themselves among the first piikani blackfoot
to ride a horse, these sacred animals
brought by the white man from far across the sea

image one is age thirteen
and already brown weasel woman, later pitamakan
demonstrates courage that is rare
when, on a buffalo hunt with her father
their small party, close to home after the hunt
her roan loaded with fresh meat
an enemy war party attacks them, then makes chase
toward our camp

while moving at top speed
her father's horse is shot and killed from under him
brown weasel woman turns and charges back
into great bursts of arrows and gunfire
rescues her father, and that, only after
she stops, dismounts, unties the fresh meat from behind her
making room for her father and their escape

image two is age fifteen when both pitamakan's parents die
her father is killed by the absaroke peoples
in a short time, her mother dies from a broken heart
brown weasel woman makes her intentions known
she'll act as both mother and father
to the younger children, her two brothers and two sisters
she'll maintain the lodge of her parents
together with suya'ki and her infant child

and so it is I paint us on the robe, to tell of our life
though not easy, beautiful and rich
for brown weasel woman's aim is always true
her intent respectful and honest and our lodge overflows
with love, with the meat and robes and leather
of buffalo and deer, antelope and elk
to share and to eat and to trade

image three is age twenty and the day arrives when
brown weasel woman saves our entire herd of horses
from capture
and in this salish raid, kills one of their men
takes his gun and his horse

the people are witness to her skill, her speed
her devotion, her fearlessness
and lone walker, who is chief at the time
honours brown weasel woman with a talk and a prayer
and it is then that her new name, pitamakan
an ancient name carried by many famous warriors before our time
is passed to her
it is then that the young warriors of a men's sacred society
approach pitamakan to become a member
an honour she modestly accepts

image four is age twenty, when on the advice of elders
pitamakan fasts and seeks a vision
four days and four nights in prayer, alone on chief mountain
the creator rewards her with a vision and the power needed
to lead a warrior's life

when she returns from chief mountain
the people consider the young pitamakan
to be a gifted one whose special powers guide her
from that day forward
only the spirits can judge and guide her

as the years pass pitamakan is seen as a holy woman
who puts up sundances, devotes herself to sun
whose flowing yellow hair informs her vision of power

image five is age twenty-four, when pitamakan insists she join
a war party against the absaroke
designed to seek revenge for her father's death
on their return she's again proclaimed to be a medicine girl
a girl chief, for she single-handedly
saves a herd of piikani blackfoot horses captured by the absaroke

image six is age thirty-three, the time of year
when the dewless air is filled with the wonder of meadowlarks
the smell of sweetgrass on the wind
a strong wind and the clouds above the mountains
white and spiralled, tell us this prairie wind
will blow like this for days

pitamakan wakes that morning and tells me of her dream
where many horses are given to her
I tell her, go, gather a party and go to the sun river
there you'll find the horses in your dream

and so it is she gathers a party of women and men
who travel on a lengthy journey
until they sight a salish camp at the sun river
come to hunt buffalo on the plain
pitamakan confides to her party, this is the reason we're here
as told to me in a dream
tonight we eat well, for by tomorrow
we'll take many horses on the long treck home

just before daybreak, they approach the salish
who sleep in their tipis in a large camp
and pitamakan swiftly tells the party, brothers and sisters
rope the horses you can from outside the camp

she tells them, I'm not good with a rope
so I'll go into the centre and see what's there
she prays to the creator and sings her power song
then walks alone among the sleeping men
one by one, she cuts loose five prize horses

then, as promised, two days and nights they ride
without sleep or food, pitamakan in the lead
and those with skill keep the ones who sleep on their horses
from falling behind
the party arrives home, tired, and dozens of horses richer

pitamakan goes straight away to the lodges of her family
gives a bay and a roan to her eldest sister
a bay and a roan to her eldest brother
and a horse to each and all her relatives

image seven is age forty-four, on the eve of her ninth raid
where pitamakan and six of her men will die
I remember my long-ago dream
where I saw her death this day
I tell her, no, don't go
pitamakan tells me, my tender sweet suya'ki
tonight I'm like an echo
blowing back
into our love
from the mountains
and the coulees

our life has been happy and complex
and my love for you is my life
creator will determine our end
is our beginning, and I will wait for you
with our loved ones
in the sandhills of forever
and all time

so it is I, germaine, am learning to listen and watch, wait and be still, laugh and cry, in ways I never imagined. the voices of these powerful two-spirit women, my sisters and my relations, my ancestors, fill my daytime like night-life dreams and I feel an awe I'm completely unable to come to terms with. I know what I need to do next, yet to actually jump down and through that hole? to actually follow that red road covered with so many quiet leaves? this takes confidence and direction. until, what? two days ago? I was just an ordinary woman driving along a prairie road during an early summer rainstorm. ahead of me were the mountains, snow-peaked still and ready to breathe out the wisdom of the tree people with compassion and great feeling. that's where I was headed, to the mountains.

and now, here I am, in the middle of a miracle and all I can do is feel like a frightened girl faced with a decision only her mother can make. what would my mother say? she'd say, smarten up. just do it. jump. what would my nokomis, my grandmother, say? she'd tell me, my girl, can't lives on won't street. you've got what it takes. and even so, even throughout my all-day struggle with jump, don't jump, jump, don't jump, that crow stays with me, leaving only for short periods of time. I find the bird's presence comforting and familiar. I know there's a reason why I'm here. I know I'm in the spirit world, and even at that, I still feel like a girl-child inside someone else's dream. I finally ask in the smallest of voices for the help and guidance of the young crow and the small spotted eagle, who have clearly presented themselves as my helpers here.

in that instant, I hear them both laugh a belly laugh, and I laugh too.
I throw down the stone and jump through the hole. I try to keep my
eyes open as I see a foothills valley at nightfall, ready for a new day, a
new season, preparing for winter. I see yellow grasses rushing into me,
bursting with reds and oranges, the colours of blood, life's sacred. in the
spring the meadowlarks nest and sing their incredible song. in the fall
it's like the grasses are their song made new again at day's end. and the
mountains. such power to hold in your hair, your skin, your eyes, and
you can drive that power home on a bus or in a car, wear that power
for days on end. I know I owe these mountains something heartfelt
and loving, a prayer of thanksgiving. and just as I'm about to land, I
hear a voice from deep within the mountains after the heat of the day
finds its way skyward. the rock calls out to the ancient ones, spilling out
fresh, long tales and delicate orange blossoms, day's end light the only
backdrop to a colour whose brilliance is the most delicate, the most
sensuous of songs.

oh, my sisters, pick up your power
my sisters, claim your voice
remember those gone before us
and pray for those yet to come

small spotted eagle:
a river of mountains whose flow is life's first
the art of prose or distant verse

there is a doorway
between those with form
and those without
the doorway is an open one
whose wind is warm
a whisper inside bone
honour those not yet born
and those
who have left you
for they live   for a time
in this place

well into the evening, when the sun is low and yellow, small spotted
eagle sees the small round stone as it's tossed out and down into the
water far below her cliff home. the water's clear and clean and fresh
water green and the stone skips, skips, skips, then floats and spreads
like a pie in the face of it all. the young crow hops through the hole in
the floor of the cave and the woman follows, grabbing at branches on
the way down in order not to just free-fall, the way is so steep. they land
together on that crow stone island, the woman and the crow—violet-
red-yellow-two-tone-blue—rolling and laughing, rolling and laughing,
just as small spotted eagle joins them. and so it begins.

the fleshly woman arrives on the tiny island, tired from her long
first day of her fast, without food and water. small spotted eagle has
waited lifetimes for this moment, and, just as she has imagined, the
fleshly woman smells wonderful, like the bellies of lilies so loved by
hummingbirds, her hair like summer sweetgrass after rain. small spotted
eagle is tired too, and, hard as it is to believe, so is the little crow. after
a day of ups and downs, even the crow is ready for a quiet rest next to
the fire he so reverently builds over the next couple hours. young crow
suggests that since some miracle has brought them all together like this,
and since small spotted eagle and the woman seem to be so well-versed in
almost perfect crow-kak, while they warm themselves they ought to share
stories about new beginnings after rain.

a chill has crept into the air. the fleshly woman is wrapped in the crow-blanket now, ready for another night of flight. from a distance they look like three moons huddled close enough to each other's secrets to stand out in a crowd. and there's the fire, whose long yellow vowels find their way into the trees like prayer cloths and promises of a sunrise reflected in the intricate veins of each winded leaf. fire's voice, full of mother's breath, a giving of permission cocooned to smooth, speaks low and slow into small spotted eagle's ear.

fire:
the kind of love that can be felt across a mountain
bloodearth red and fire in the same bed

I am fire   bringer of renewal   inside out   to be
one with me   is to be my sister   I present the
doubts   the red-faced wonder   to the ancestors   who
hold fire as their child   give what you no longer need to the
fire spirit my children   where there's hope   doubt's
gentler resting place

a misty rain
new moon and long before dawn
ponder the power of sun
a quiet wonder
under kindled dreams
a wishing well
and still the morning waits
on the other side
of rain

I look inside and I see
bright as fire
a youth lying there
where only yesterday
there were bones
dried by sun

I am fire   inside fire there is rain   learn what there
is to learn there   sacred knowing   waits   sun on water
smoulders the unseen   know this   with every
sunrise   the power of the sun's light empowers your spirit and gives you
life   trust   those who dare to look inside her light
water   quenches   deep into the mother

the way you stretch your face   onto the roundness of a spoon
and there   a note pinned onto a door   those who believe
they can do something   and those who believe they cannot
            are both right

gopher (with one eff):
water birds on hockey rinks
and the mountains just moments away

letter to germaine:

i dreamed throughout the night last night, and days of nights now, of
a heavy, heavy silence, a force that's powerful and malevolent and alive,
like weendigo, whose greed is so great, whose hunger can't be satisfied
and grows rather than wanes when fed.

like that monster weendigo, the silence hates with a passion that hurts,
like sand blowing on the body, on the face, with the full force of
a southern prairie wind storm. no germaine to hold hands with. no feet
to follow. just this massive, powerful, hungry wind that grows with
its own fulfillment, pushing and pulling at everything in its path.

yet, through it all, my eyes are able to take in everything, protected by
the lenses of my sunglasses. the dreams are so overpowering, so real.
which is why i'm writing all this down, to hold close what the old ones
tell us, namely that each grandmother and grandfather is here for the
next, to smooth the ground.

i look outside and there's water dripping from the sides of houses now,
wonderful and clear, slowly freezing and growing with the gentleness
of shade. around the corner is peace, a bank of snow overflowing with
children in snow clothes sucking long, clear icicles, chatting and biting
and sucking and feeling good on a cold, sunny day. after weeks of living
inside a kind of transparent frozen home, like an icicle, where water—
life—held all my secrets, my body's fragrance, like berries and spice, has
been held there. i'm safe now, to lift my arms from their place, frozen to
my sides, and now i've written you a poem, like a shopping list,
but different.

the teachings say adult two-spirit people are presumed to be
generous, exceptional, intellectual
artistic, healers, people of power
mediators, singers, interpreters of dreams
kind and dedicated to children, devoted to the welfare of the group

love forever,
gopher (with one eff)

young crow:
that beautiful mountain and the sea in her face
not an e or an i to stand on

in case you don't already know, this is me, young crow talking. I dream inside my mind there's an unfamiliar face. now, being I'm not the intellectual type, I check a mirror, and sure enough, there's some bird staring back, fools hen body with big peacock breath. the offer is there, so off I go, and before I know what's up what's down, some chicken's planting red corn seed in the median of the highway. I'm ready to go out and start the car to go to the gym when I notice there's a cat, a pig and a duck playing scrabble in the back, keeping an eye on the hen, and just when I'm convinced I'm awake and losing it, I have a dream that wakes me up for real on this, the second day of the fleshly woman's fast.

I guess I'm making so much noise with my kak-kaking in my sleep, everyone in earshot's distance is wide awake, so maw-caw shakes me, wakes me up and coos at me, you've been having bad dreams, my boy. fly and by I tell her I feel like I'm going soft. she tells me, I might be on to something.

maw-caw says, if people had wings and black feathers, few of them would be clever enough to be crows, except maybe them métis. so now you know, she tells me, now you know that fleshly woman over there's one of them métis. that's what those dreams of yours are telling you, my boy. nothing more nothing less. wherever you see a crow, my boy, you'll see the métis. we got lots in common. for example, exactly nine months after the white man comes to turtle island, we both start to grow like corn on a hill of beans, squash and melons all around us.

now, I'm not trying to paint the picture red, but after facing two of my fearsomest fears kak-to-kak—heights and confined, confounded spaces, a.k.a. caves? today I decide to rest. at least I've got a full belly from in that cave. turns out, out of the bluest of blues, there was a hubcap stuck just under the fleshly woman's blanket, shining out like the moon, and stuck in every crack and crevice of that hubcap was one of them deliciously delicate little deerflies, their bellies puffed out with blood, like straight out of reality TV.

we're still on this little crow-stone island we landed on. someone has left enough firewood to last for days, and somehow, someway, the grandmother cottonwood from over on the plains has rooted herself right here too. the fleshly woman spends her day mostly in prayer and learning, and from the looks of things, she didn't sleep a wink last night. she's been walking a lot, like she's trying to walk off something deep and bone-heavy.

after what happened yesterday inside that rock, the woman knows the mountains will always cleanse and save her from herself. now she knows you can let go of all the negative stresses there and at the water beds. and all this just before I hear the fleshly woman say something like, a lifetime of dreaming myself whole, one small bird at a time. now, that gets my attention in the late afternoon sun, and seeings she's looking right at me when she talks, I'm convinced I'm her intended audience. so I keep my ears open and my kak shut.

her words are long and bookish, but I think I hear her say, hundreds of thousands of years of two-spirit women and, just like that, safety is something in stories and glorious moments outdoors, and that's what we'll recover there, is the magic of the she-he, the magic of the he-she.

the fleshly woman tells me—or at least I think she's telling me—this morning I could feel the heat from the fire and I know she's my sister, warm and welcoming—the bringer of renewal. she continues, I've had so many dreams where fire has dramatically and emphatically changed my life—my inner life—and my outer life changes instantly.

I'm like the fire spirit, she says. like air and water, light and shade, and the fire spirit works slowly to reveal my intended path. I carry the fire with me now, like the little crow in his story, a piece of cottonwood kept hot by a sacred fire, my sister-friend, calling my name in the open wind.

and today? says the fleshly woman. after a sleepless night? all I want to do is walk. I don't ever remember feeling such a need to walk, to move myself forward and feel the mother in my body, her heartbeat in my legs, my hips, my eyes. I cry and I pray and I walk, a stream of conscious thought that wants to straddle the other side of sight and sound and touch. to feel my own knowing, my birthright. why else am I here? continues the fleshly woman, her eyes full of rain.

just when I'm about to answer with some wise kak or another, she goes on as if I'm not even there. she starts up with a kind of whisper, low to the ground, and I can barely hear her say something like, first and foremost is respect. respect, and to be sincere, to be discreet, humble. to be silent and to listen. to love, knowing both good and bad medicine exist at one and the same time and place and space. she hums now, short rhythmic bursts, her voice like a baby bird's.

that's it. that's all she says all day. goes on to walk and pray the day away. me? after the last couple days I feel like one of those small birds who survives the bitter cold, song shrill and beautiful at the end of the day, carrying far across to the other side of the river, his voice a reminder of the way the cold can make the longest whisper sound loud and close, even when the distance can't be flown in a half-hour.

as maw-caws would say, in that kind of cold, moments become life, and I'm reminded of a story told to me by an old crow during my first winter in the city. I was lost and I couldn't find the maw-caws. loud as I cawed, all's I heard was the heartbeat of mother earth through a concrete statue of sitting bull, and it's then that I felt the warm wing of an old crow lull me rock me hold me hum.

but it wasn't no old crow at all, it was the reassuring hand of none other than the one, the only, shirley bear, out and about, rollerblading into her seventies, her wisdom from the southward way for us all to hear on day two. shirley bear, her long, silver hair moving sideways in the light, the wind dry and sending her sweet red scent skyward, up to the clouds and around the early evening stars.

and behind shirley bear, woman chief, a'aninin woman from the past, who tells her story then, the mountains rising all around her like mother earth's backbone straining to keep her safe. their words are like grass after fire, filling the air with charcoal and dust, powder spreading away from the centre of the flames in one swift motion. what's left is a song, next year's glory, a green so green, the burnt black is but a memory of words making themselves heard from the soles of tired feet.

shirley bear recites the southward path
her poem from *virgin bones:*
belayak kcikug'nas'ikn'ug
"the vocation of storytelling"

the winds from the south caressingly breathe
warm red ochre on her sister
the earth
which melts the ice and snow
that has covered this tired sister during a short rest

the melting ice creates
a waking song
heard by sleeping animals
birds
fish
insects and crawling things

it wakes the plant life
which sustains the men
women and children

at the southern direction comes another story
listen to the daughter and caretaker of the red pipestone
listen to her story

the second day her intruders start to play with her bones
the sun is hot and her bones become very dry
thirst dances provocatively before her
tempting
tantalizing
urging her to quench

I am pine leaf, later known as woman chief, a'aninin woman
here again to talk in a more serious way, to clarify
for there are several gender choices
at least there were until the arrival of the white man

I was captured by the absaroke when I was still a girl
my childhood name was barcheeampe, pine leaf
I was born not long after a smallpox epidemic
all but decimated my people

early in childhood, my twin brother was killed
during a piikani raid, and while still deep in grief
I was captured by the absaroke, adopted by an absaroke man who'd
lost his wife to illness, his three sons to conflicts with the piikani

an astute and kind man, my father supported my preference
for boyhood games and pursuits
in time, I became known as a fearless horseback rider
equally skilled with a rifle
though I dressed like the girls and women of my time

we're told we all have two sides, the female and the male
the female side is the left, closest to our life blood
our heart
the right side is the male

upon adulthood, most people seek a companion
in order to bring a spiritual balance
to their female and male sides
thus completing themselves, the female in the male
balancing with the female in the woman
the male in the woman, balancing with the male in the man

this is the kind of union the white man enforced among his people
before, and after his arrival to this land
as his judeao-christian religions dictate, without heart
and mindlessly label the union of the two-spirits an abomination

I was considered a capital shot with the rifle
and I spent a good deal of my time killing deer and bighorn
which I butchered and carried home on my back
when hunting on foot, as my father taught me

so too my father boasted me to be equal, if not superior
to any of the men in hunting, both on foot and horseback
where I was able to take down four or five buffalo at a race
cut up the animals on my own, bringing the meat and hides home

from an early age, songs resounded my praise
after many brave deeds
I attacked and killed full-grown grizzly bears, alone
and as a successful hunter I shared my meat freely

yet times have changed
the shame and fear of the two-spirits
throughout the communities today
comes from the white man's shame
before and after they arrived on this continent

once they reached our homeland, turtle island
these poor young white men followed their fathers before them
who slaughtered more than ten million women
their mothers, wives, sisters, cousins, grandmothers, aunties, friends

turning their women and girls in to the authorities, as witches
for a couple hundred years
this was normal for them, familiar, expected, everyday
so that by the time they arrived here, that's what they knew

after my father's death, I assumed control of his lodge, as was his wish
and I performed the double duty of father and mother
to the other children
too, I took as my wife, in the ways of the absaroke people
my people now, a woman I'd loved deeply for years
and I offered horses to her parents
after we pledged our love for one another

we shared all manner of interests
considered those of both women and men
a few years later, I took four more wives
who shared their wealth and talents freely

following the treaty of laramie
the six of us
became active negotiators for peace
among the nations of the upper missouri
and we gathered fame in this way
as traders and warriors, our successes demonstrating
the power of our medicine, our personal bravery

while at the same time, over there in europe
women were still being stoned to death
dismembered and quartered
the diameter of their clitorises, measured and recorded
their breasts brutally hacked away
before they were burned at the stake

not popular history, these facts
not like the pirates and explorers, anthropologists and priests
the inventors of things, but history nonetheless
history they like to bury deep outside themselves
a shame that festers like a mildew
but even bleach, even arsenic or lye
couldn't control what this one's done

healing
is the only way
to change

contrary to what some people may think
of women who love women
none of myself nor my wives were quick to quarrel
we loved to fool around, appreciated all people, young and old
lived a good life with our children

when a party of piikani attacked our village
as before, I killed several of the enemy, while escaping injury myself
the absaroke people began to believe mine was a charmed life
and with my daring feats
I was elevated to a point of honour and respect
not often reached by either male or female warriors

now this is not to say we
us natives, us inuit, us métis
are a bunch of saints and angels
walking around on top of the water here on turtle island

not at all
we have our strengths, our shortcomings, our problems
like anybody
and we can't turn back

the good old north american clock
tic-tock
tic-tock
tic-tock

to my great surprise and honour
when the tribal council was held and all the chiefs assembled
I took my place among them
as the third-highest-ranked person of one hundred sixty lodges
and at a council of the absaroke and the cree
I was asked to sit in fifth place among the absaroke chiefs

for twenty years I conducted myself well in all things
then suddenly and instantly, the white man's gold rush began
and with it the influx of more than one hundred thousand
fortune-hunters driven by greed

aware now of the immediate need
for unity among the nations
I led an absaroke peacekeeping mission
to my native a'aninin people
but resentful after my previous raids
some of the a'aninin men trapped and killed me
my death saddening and enraging the absarokes so that they refused
to make peace with the a'aninin for many years

now, it's well into the second night of the fleshly woman's fast, and I'm warming by the fire—me, young crow—and small spotted eagle over there. the fleshly woman, still awake, is sitting finally. I'm staring into the fire between kak-naps, composing airy poetry.

voices sweet inside a southerly breeze
their tones pulling, fragrant and lush
between song and sound

eyes that see forever
their vision—firelight, making its way
lyrical and new

whose long-winded view
caught inside a cloud
in the shape of a tune

incites a knowledge
inward-facing
waiting

at the end of the day, I wonder why the tiny birds are playing under the piano when there's the whole outdoors and I wonder, too, what kind of wood makes the most pleasing sounds? then I remember, if you want to change the shape of a thing? wing it. sing at the top of your lungs.

tranquilized and dribbled line by line
one tired tea leaf at a time

germaine:
or dare I ask, what kind of leaf is this
the answer being implied in the question

to call the beginning of the third day of my fast abrupt would be a gross
understatement. I say this with utter calmness now, but at the time I felt
almost overwhelmed with emotions I can't begin to describe. though
I didn't realize I'd fallen asleep, it turns out I woke myself up—with
my own out-loud voice while talking to a wolf in a dream. to my utter
pleasure and relief, shirley bear was there again, her beautiful smile
reassuring me, reminding me that today I'm to learn the lessons from
the west.

shirley bear, maliseet woman of today
who sees creator's beauty everywhere
in the tar and concrete rooftops
on the faces and shapes of women
who grace vancouver's east end

shirley bear, who plants herself like a sugar maple
solid and cycling steep mountainsides
up from the sea and onto the wet, blue hills

where she recites the westward path
her poem from *virgin bones*:
belayak kcikug'nas'ikn'ug
"the vocation of storytelling"

the west winds bear down on the earth
and all its relations
with the black grandmother clouds
who bring the thunder and rain

she pours the water on her sister
which heals
cleanses and nourishes
all the relations
who walk on her

listen to the thundering words
of her story

earlier in the dream, just before seeing shirley bear, I'd been visiting
an old medicine woman at her lodge. she was teaching me and other
women, wordlessly, and we were able to understand her thoughts. she
turned her head towards her friend, a young woman, who began to
speak slowly in her language, michif, quiet and serious.

I'm called claude sauvageaux dit lafrance
métisse woman
this is what I know of masahai matkwisa manye
alluring young girl who is pleasing
mohave woman, a woman made wealthy
from doctoring and from her hard work as a farmer and hunter
she's known to be very lucky when it comes to finding women lovers
which I would know, being I'm one of the lesser known
in her later years

I wear a black velvet jacket tied at the waist with a métis sash
on the back of my jacket I've embroidered the mark of my people
the infinity symbol, white on blue, and below that the mark of me
the face of a broken heart, violet-red-yellow-two-tone-blue

I travel a long distance, to california and mexico from the north
to help return four hundred head of breeding stock
but I stay along the way after I meet masahai matkwisa manye
when I hear her dreams give her the most powerful
of skills, for she is able to cure sexual diseases

I have such an infection, painful and raw
since my girlhood, when my uncle's wine-teared bristles
chafe my tender thighs, my soft pink places rawed to purplegreen
holes burned around my secrets
under the quilted stars

I learn to hide my life behind my eyes, to show no fear, no terror
not every time, but enough to hold my spirit
like a strand of rich silk ribbon
around my face

so when I meet masahai matkwisa manye, she much older than me
my heart holds moments of unspoken pain
frozen there, for otherwise I would die from the very release
of the trauma, as such utter voilation of the spirit is so rare
among the métis

she tells me, like me, her brother's vicious force
beats her neck her breasts her whole, drags her behind a bush
and brutally defiles her sacred places
so that even she, a fully adult woman of much known power
suffers years of paining hate against herself
as such voilence is so rare, too, among the mohave

she looks my way and, through that parchment
the skin on her eyes, strips clarity unevened
hushes silence, doubtful proud and longing hope
the grandmothers dancing silver moons
where easy smiles and strong brown tea
mingle laughter's love

masahai matkwisa manye reaches out to me
touches my bird-boned hands, nails chewed down to the quick
early-feared and night-shy, pain-ready to take flight
through the eye of a needle

she starts to become like vapour, goes upside down and through
a small hole in the water, and gently—very, very gently
takes, touches my face, palms full on my cheeks
fingers pressed upward, pulls me into the hole
through to stone and tree, doorways
where water looks inside

so it is I'm cured of this dreaded disease
by masahai matkwisa manye

and water is where she meets her ancestors soon after
for by brutal force, her male lover and his friend
while drunk and boasting, beat her unconscious
then throw her into the colorado river, where she drowns
only to be found two weeks later
she's then cremated in the traditional way
of the mohave people

and me, my oil-warmed woman palms
vein of earth and story hems the line
hooked bound and pages side to side
a rocking chair of cherry wood
our gifts from the grandmothers
whose healing songs are woven in
red and in our hands
clear-throated sound vibrations
healing songs

grandma moon, sister sun
mother earth, we are one
let us move, to heal the earth
know the moon, touch the sun
heal as one

as claude sauvageaux dit lafrance comes to the end of her story, the old
lady begins to sing the healing song, powerful and long. she teaches the
song to all of us there, and tells us we're sisters of the spirit of the water
here. after a time, she takes my hand and walks with me back to the
grandmother cottonwood on this crow-stone island, tells me my spirit
will have more than enough water to meet my commitments here, that
I can call on her any time, no matter where I might be. she shows me
where I am, and I'm able to see myself in the tree and on a mountain.
she tells me she's my mother, that the water spirit here has adopted me
as her sister and she lives in me now, is part of me, that I am a water
woman. she tells me to go to the places in my life where I've prayed
by water and I spend many days in dream time, going to these places,
offering tobacco and giving thanks.

when I wake from my dreams, I'm more than a little surprised to find
myself—height-leery and bladder-full—sitting on a tiny branch, very
high up in the cottonwood. I'm stunned as I sit there, petrified of
heights, my legs dangling, hoping I'm still asleep.

within seconds, I'm surrounded by tiny lights. at first I think they're
aphids and they become frightened when I think this. then I realize
they can't be aphids, I'm up far too high, and they begin to touch me,
to caress me, to tell me I'm doing the right thing, I'll be all right. I pray
to the grandmothers and the water spirit shows herself and reminds me
she's my sister.

I tell her I need to be held and she holds me like a child, rocking me
in her arms while she stands on the branch of the tree, her feet like a
crow's. she's wonderful and green and smells like rain. she tells me I'll be
okay, I'll learn about myself and how I can serve the ancestors and my
community as a two-spirit woman. she sings to me in a quiet

soothing voice, rocks me in her arms, back and forth, back and forth, then tosses me out into the open air from the top of that grandmother tree.

gopher (with one eff):
do i sleep, which rhymes with leaf
a question put only for literary effect

letter to germaine:

after i wrote to you last time, i went ahead and just felt, nothing held
back or tucked behind my ear. i felt pretty good at the end of the day,
when winter finally arrived and i fell into sleep. i'd never been so ready
for winter, and here i just woke up and we're having a false spring.
there's a chinook arch out there that looks like a snowy owl at full
moon, stretched into forever. so, i thought, i'm up now, i may as well
write to you again before winter and sleep return their grace. i checked
the date on my computer and i realize you left us for the spirit world
three months ago now. three months and it feels like three hundred
years.

but, after a good solid sleep, i feel more mature somehow, if that makes
any sense. i'm in my chamber holding my own beauty close, like the air
here, opening herself, words on a page, full of hope and mystery, waiting
for a moment, just that most perfect of moments, when movement is a
song, sacred and hollowed out from rain-shaped stone.

water and
wind
and fire's blossom
fine
fine breath
afternoons and reading all day long

not bad for a hole-in-the-grounder, hey? you know, i was fortunate
enough to witness the crows gather this fall, early and very loud. i
tried to hear what they were saying, and sometimes i think i did. there
was this one crow, a natural leader, who kept looking down my home
hole and leaving fluffs of kleenex and shiny bits from a palm-pilot. i
remembered you telling me when a crow visits, pay attention, you're
being visited by magic. crows have cross-eyed three-dee vision, you said,
cuz they can see what's going on in the present, the past and the future

—all at the same time. they keep one foot in this world and one in the world of the invisibles. i thought i heard him say never-door or nearer-more or four-on-the-floor, i just wasn't sure.

but that was months ago, and now there's a wind inside the house. not a big wind, but the kind of wind that carries spring's promise and the air inside that wind is cool and clear. there's a light on the floor, and i'm told there are january water birds on the field floods, behaving like characters in a badly written novel that's lost its own fiction so's the story, the characters themselves, take over and defy their limits, leaping from the edges of the page. wherever you are today, germaine, my love is there, watery and round.

gopher (with one eff)

young crow:
do I please, do I persuade
do leaves do

I dream I'm a small bird playing hopscotch on the back of some
woman's shirt, ribbons hanging all around, violet-red-yellow-two-tone-
blue. there are delicate, tiny birds all around me, nervous about my
presence, awake constantly, standing up in their nests in alarm because
the young ones can't breathe, can't leave, and they're yelling at me to
stop, stop! they've taught me to juggle my eyeballs, you see, and even
though they've explained carefully that there are limits to the length
of time this fun can go on before you lose your eyes for good, another
sabotage of the fleshly woman, is what I think. then I wake up, one eye
in mid-air and the other stuck in the mud, its edges gnawed by mice. try
and sleep after a dream like that.

as you might've already guessed, this is me, young crow talking,
hoodwinked by the glitter of my own gadgets. as soon as I wake up
and check my eye sockets for eyeballs and take a look around, I start
to panic. the fleshly woman's gone, kakked clean away. I flap around,
flailing, trying to remember something maw-caws say about how one
of crow's gifts is we know people's thoughts and we've got that three-dee
vision thing. whatever a person might be thinking? wherever a person
might be? we can tell. trick is, though, it's important to stay calm, and,
well, I don't feel too calm right now, so I check my blackberry just in
case. nope. either the fleshly woman's stopped thinking, or my crow-
know's on the blink. don't get me wrong, I have no qualms about my
abilities. why else live? it's just that waking up to a disappeared fleshly
woman is definitely not what I expected on this fine fall summery day.
this is the third day of her fast and it's my job to watch out for her.

it's then, in mid-thought, that I see the notes, waving at me like double
vision, one pinned neatly to a branch at the top of the tree and one
peeking out from the slope of the sand. I can't believe I didn't see them
sooner, and, me being me, first I hippiddy-hop on over to the note
nearby before I fly on up there so close to the sky. I have to tug, to dig
and tug on that note pushed deep into the hard, packed sand. I dig and
tug until my pedicure gets ruined, and still no go. so, I decide to check

out the note way up in the tree. I recognize the writing right away. it has
to belong to small spotted eagle. it's intense and powerful, with an edge,
a hardness, like bumping up against thick biceps hidden inside a baggy
short-sleeved shirt on a small-waisted woman. and I would know.
the note is long and goes onto the other side of the page. the note reads
like so.

one crow tomorrow, be sure to collect her things
the baskets and the medicines, the knapsack
crow blanket and small stone
round and lovely on this autumny sunny day

four crows a test, go south and west
of you know where, and there
at kak-kak's very own nest we'll be
now turn the note over and you'll see
how clever even a small spotted eagle can be

and here, where mystery shakes her hair like an ad on tv
water tracks her longing to the rows of precious ribbon
as she reads her sisters' bloodlines in the filaments of silk

unravelling her fingers strand by braided strand
red sash and velvet dresses draws her back to blood and bones
whose daughters tracing lifetimes, holds her blanket from her face

well I'll be a kak's cradle, I think. couldn't've done better myself. now I
know where to find the fleshly woman and small spotted eagle. at crow
mountain. as I'm reading the note that's written in kak-code again just
to be sure, this time out loud, out of the corner of my eye I can see that
the other note's blown itself free from the sand, only to catch an updraft,
spiralling to a speck within seconds. so I face my fears and I surprise
myself cuz I feel dizziness, not dread, as I fly so high into the sky I
almost throw up last week's flybread. worth the risk in the end, though,

cuz on that very old paper, preserved by the hot dry sand, there's
a poem, written in tiny round letters—like music—by none other
than the notable susette bright-eyes lafleshe, omaha two-spirit woman
from a time long passed, who was well-known for her flair with words,
titled, composing poetry stops the horses.

morning and night the white woman
for whom I work
writes of the indian question
the mighty movement of american civilization
of manifest destiny's inevitable goal
of the white man's role to americanize
to sanitize, revolutionize
to genocide what's left of the indians
these primitive relics of man's ancient past, at last
coaxed into the inevitable
evolution of the white man's supremacy
over all other nations, his superior physical capacities
and mental libations a cut above the rest
when put to the test, bubonic plague, smallpox, influenza
tuberculosis, common cold
kills indians off in numbers untold
and though anglo ranchers and miners deprave
the laws of the new world will pervade

what the white woman for whom I work
doesn't write
is how now it's the white man's lawful right
to hunt, to kill, to slaughter

any indian woman and her infant daughter
son, husband, cousin, mother, father
grandmother, grandfather
seen anywhere on this land
or by any water's sand

small spotted eagle:
another, dare I ask, in leaf
while still in the womb

what you send out in every instance comes back to you a thousand-fold.
changing what you think of yourself will change the whole of you. other
people will see and feel this and change will be stimulated in them.
the elderly elders' attitude promotes this kind of ripple effect. it fills you
up, overflows, and then reaches out to touch and change the rest of
the world.

these are her thoughts as small spotted eagle moves into earshot of the
women on the ground. they show themselves to the fleshly woman in
person now, as in her dreams, in order to keep her spirit-memory sharp.
they've chosen another mountain on her third day—crow mountain—
to share their stories, past and present. the old lady from the fleshly
woman's dream is here, telling the women who sit around her, these
days folks are conditioned to simply accept what they perceive to be
their limitations.

trying to break out of the mold that's been created by centuries of terror
is not unlike little birds hiding under the sheets, window wide open, and
what can they do? yet little birds always have something to sing—and
they will sing—their songs sacred and changing the lives of everyone.
if you pay attention, you'll see that little birds will sing until their voices
hurt their words, and only then will they sit down quietly and make a
drawing of their love.

small spotted eagle wants to share this moment with that hokey-pokey
crow, but earlier today she isn't able to rouse him from sleep, not when
the fleshly woman goes airborne, and not when she returns to get him
after the woman is settled on the southwest side of crow mountain in a
secluded spot. so small spotted eagle writes a clever note in crow-code
she knows he'll appreciate. now—here at crow mountain—there are
several women sitting in a circle on blankets and cushions. they've built
a fire and they're talking quietly, each woman speaking in her turn,
passing an eagle feather from one woman to the next.

small spotted eagle is looking forward to witnessing the women, and as she waits in the peace of this place for the hip-hop crow to show, she's amazed that just a few hours ago she thought the woman would meet her fleshly death here after all. that way, all the fleshly woman learned here in the world of the invisibles would remain here for now, and the ancient ones would wait again. small spotted eagle remembers the exact thought that was moving from her heart to her head when she woke up with a start after hearing a heavy, heavy silence just above her, near the top of the cottonwood on that crow-stone island retreat.

in fact, she was still in mid-thought—a lovely thought—when, there, right at eye-level, she saw the fleshly woman, mid-air, no crow blanket, cocooned inside thousands of tiny dew-beads, shimmering violet-red-yellow-two-tone-blue with the early morning light. a human falls at a rate of three hundred kilometres an hour when pencil-straight, one-hundred-eighty when making like a bird in flight. either way, without intervention, without help, neither free-fall nor flight from this height is an option for the humans, even on this side of things. small spotted eagle was just about to offer her back to the fleshly woman when the dew performed like rain and fire, wind and song, and carried the fleshly woman to crow mountain to set her down among these two-spirit women.

the women are well into their talking circle when the little crow finally arrives, wearing headphones and elbow pads, his back bent under the weight of the baskets, his eye-pod sticking out from among the fleshly woman's things. the story told next is a long one, that of qanqon kamek klaula, sitting-in-the-water-grizzly, from the akuklaho, the meadow valley people of the lower kutenai, as told by three of her partners over the span of her adult life. they tell of her life in four parts, parts three and four being told by the same woman. each part represents a time of deep growth and transformation for qanqon kamek klaula.

the first woman who speaks is wrapped in her blanket, her small brown hands reaching out between the folds in constant motion with her words. she tells of certain natural occurances that signal the end of things as we know them, one such event being the fall of volcanic ash that created a blanket deeper than a yearling goose over their homeland, making their hunters lucky for several days as deer were tracked in the ash. young crow settles onto small spotted eagle's back and they listen together, the crow and the eagle, to the voices of the women who grace the side of this mountain on this warm, sunny day.

that same year the mountain erupts its secrets over the land
is the year of qanqon kamek klaula's birth
of mine and the women after me
who become long-time lovers and companions
to one standing-lodge-pole-woman, ququnok
later known as gone-to-the-spirits, kauxuma nupika
and later still as sitting-in-the-water-grizzly, qanqon kamek klaula
from the akuklaho, the meadow valley people of the lower kutenai

we'll tell this story in four equal parts
our dust resting on our backs
as we speak of matters difficult and dear to us
yet as the dust remains centuries into the future
so our stories speak today of spirals into living rooms
and shared knowledge of our mothers yet to come

I know of standing-lodge-pole-woman throughout my youth
her beauty heavy on her frame, even then she's called manlike
and though her fine long hands resemble mine
we're different in every other way

when our young womanhood arrives
at the same time as the influx of the white man's fur trade
one standing-lodge-pole-woman leaves with a frenchman
a manservant, and I marry a man who fishes
in our home waters

for over a year she's away, winters at kootenae house
where she learns she's skilled with languages
speaks cree, french and english while she lives in the mountains
at the north side of lake windermere with the manservant
before returning home to her people from this most violent of men

upon her homecoming, she claims
the manservant performs an operation to transform her to a man
her words are remembered in this way
I'm a man now, is what she says
we kutenai did not believe the white people
possessed such power from the supernaturals
I can tell you that they do, greater power than we have
they changed my sex while I was with them
no kutenai is able to do that

she changes her name to kauxuma nupika
gone-to-the-spirits, and when she comes upon people
she performs a dance, a gesture of her man-self
her claim to male pursuits and habits
oh, to see her dressed in leggings and breech cloths
men's shirts and my, oh my
more beauty was never seen here in this part of the land

as time goes by, she carries a gun, a bow and arrows
and expresses her wish to marry a woman
she makes advances on several young unmarried women
she is refused, until one night on pine island
when lying inside a young woman's lodge
as is the custom

the young woman, afraid and thoroughly undone
runs to the lodge of a relative and in the morning
when gone-to-the-spirits emerges, I appear before her
having left my people along the kootenay river
to make a home with her

we two are now to be seen
as constant companions and many are curious
to know what secrets are hidden inside her leggings
they tell me, tell us what's there
but me I laugh my most gracious laugh each and every time

soon though, poisoned by fear in the white man's world
with outside scars mirrored inward, her temperament
hard and quick to rage
my laughter prompts a jealous streak beyond the everyday

gone-to-the-spirits creates a fiction, an affair
between myself and a male friend
begins to lift her hand her fist her knee, to beat me
to throw me up against a tree, to gamble at duck creek
and when she loses her bow, her arrows, our bark canoe

I pick up a nearby bow and let go an arrow
through the side of the canoe
I know then, I must go home to my people
for we cannot change those we love who are brutal
we can only escape them
and if by some miracle they're to be transformed
it won't be by us

I'm the second woman to become
a long-term lover of qanqon kamek kaula
I'm no longer a young woman, nor am I old
like my grandmother before me, I am a kind and quiet woman
strong and compassionate, intelligent
and I'm told I have a wisdom that's rare for my age
that my hair is my greatest source of beauty
exquisite and long

there's a time in my youth, when my grandmother
my teacher in life and in the healing ways
dies
in fact she's gone most of the day
without a breath or any sign of life
and we begin the preparations after death

then towards the end of that most difficult of days
my grandmother regains consciousness
only to tell of many days of travels along a road
where she comes upon two monstrous animals
she becomes so terrified, she turns back
and on her turning she's advised by someone unseen
to return home
she's told the number of years she'll live before her body's true death

then she's given a spirit song and a new name
and she returns to us
then much later she dies as she's advised
at the end of the years she's assigned

in our way, the spirits of the dead travel
towards the setting sun and to prepare the gift of the human body
to return to mother earth, three stripes
red, blue and yellow, are painted on either side of the person's head
to honour the three supreme beings, the akinakat
who determine the end of the world, at which time
the spirits of the dead will advance from the east
and people will once again be with their relatives and friends

in keeping with this knowledge, we kutenai share in the prophet dance
and in a roundabout way this is how I come to meet up
with gone-to-the-spirits, to become her second wife
soon after my grandmother's death
by now gone-to-the-spirits has taken an interest in matters of raids
to test her courage, and I meet her on the excersion
when she takes her final name, qanqon kamek klaula
sitting-in-the-water-grizzly

we're a fishing people, a hunting people
a people who gather medicines and herbs
and we would leave the quarrelsome-natured ones to their own
except that now, since the white man's presence
there's a greater need for such warriors
such men and women among us

our masculine ideal, not that of a bold warrior
but a skilled fisher and hunter
predominates still in our forest home
horses are not needed here as they are on the plains

nonetheless, we do learn some of the strategies of battle
used by our eastern neighbours, including the use of horses
in order to survive past and recent raids
the first excursion of gone-to-the-spirits is against the kalispel
and though an unsuccessful venture, this series of events
is what prompts both our coming together and our end

I'm gathering medicines when a small group arrives on the path
whose presence is respectfully announced by their leader
he tells me, earlier that same day, he walked through his village
to announce his purpose and direction, to steal horses
at this, I volunteer to join the group
as I have an interest in this goal
and because I'm known among these men for my successes
during such raids with my band, I'm invited along

our party journeys south and west, and after several days
of sighting neither the kalispel nor their horses
we decide to go back towards home
we cross the pen d'oreille river, begin our return on the north side
and though we pass a kalispel camp, we see no one

on excursions such as this, when we come to a body of water
a river or a stream
the group wades across in clusters, and in this way
we protect ourselves from possible attack
at these times I and the other women go just behind the first group
then dress in private
while the second group crosses
yet, today there is no danger, so I cross alone

curiously, there's a man who insists on hanging back
to cross after me
his purpose, he says, is to ensure my safety
as I'm the only woman in this raid
even when I assure him his is an unnecessary precaution
as our paths haven't crossed with the enemy
he lags behind and becomes even more persistent
so that when his catching up begins to hold up our progress
he's asked to cross with the first group
but being stubborn, with great fanfare, he refuses to agree
his brother, who is also among us, is asked to intervene

at the next crossing, a shallow one
I see that the brother waits behind the group
he crouches low, and just when I think he pauses there
to talk some sense into his brother
he suddenly runs back into the stream, and as this odd behaviour
both delays my progress and displays my nakedness
I move behind a larger bush for privacy
it's from an opening there that I witness a most marvellous sight

in the middle of the stream, is a woman
the man known as gone-to-the-spirits is, in body, a woman
half-dressed myself, I'm so amazed
I move out from behind my hiding place to get a better view

just the night before I tell this man, this gone-to-the-spirits
if he were not a man but a woman instead
his persistent advances, his charm, his wit, his loveliness
would be welcome on my part
and here all along she's all the woman I've ever dreamed for me

147

it's clear from her paining face, gone-to-the-spirits
has caught her foot between two rocks
which causes her to fall at a dangerous angle into the water
she is sitting now and in great pain, and rather than go to her side
her brother, face red and holding rage at bay
turns his back and leaves

and so begins our love, as I go to her in the water
caress her swelling ankle, broken clean through the bone
I pray and apply medicines and water in the way I'm taught
and soon her ankle bone is healed to the point
where only the blue-black swelling and tenderness remain
with me, she limps back to our waiting companions

a moment's glance tells me her brother knows
the well-kept secret of her sex
though I don't yet know the whole, I mind myself, my growing love
for this mysterious woman, whose need to be a man
far outweighs my understanding

the following day when we reach lake pen d'orielle
and we know we're safe, we stop to hunt ducks
to have a good meal before our return home
where no victory song will be sung in our honour

we've become close during our time together
and we cheer our leader, who, though down-hearted
asks if anyone would like to select a new name
only gone-to-the-spirits accepts this offer and as her story of her injury
unfolds itself around her, I'm left unmentioned
as is her broken bone, and though she describes
her brother's presence as the cause of her sitting in the water
she fails to relate his anger when he witnesses her womanness

148

she declares instead that she's happy
despite the injury that forced her to sit down in the stream
and from this day forward she wishes to be called
qanqon kamek klaula, sitting-in-the-water-grizzly

all except her brother cheer her, his actions clear
and as if to forewarn me, he looks me in the eye and speaks
his words, low and full of sting, directed to his friends
he'll use only the term qanqon, he says
a mocking of qanqon kamek klaula
and he insists he'll never use this new name
as it's meaningless and self-aggrandizing
intended to hide a bitter shame

after this event, I move to her village
into her lodge, and though my family warns me
that to begin a love this way, based on such deceit and cunning
is not what my grandmother would want for me
I thank them for their words and heartfelt tears, and I go

I don't stay longer than five full years
for soon qanqon kamek klaula displays such jealousy
I'm left wondering where she leaves those parts of herself
I desire so, her zest for life, her certainty
her laugh, her joy, her rare keen mind
blinded by a rage so pure, I insist we camp in the family group

then one night in the midst of an irrational rage
when she threatens to beat me, her brother hears her
and comes out of his lodge
he's heard enough, he says, and he calls out her name
qanqon, qanqon, qanqon, is all he says
and the quarrel ceases at once

yet her brother continues filling the quiet night air
for all the village to hear
you are hurting your woman friend, he cries
you've hurt other friends in the same way
you know that I saw you standing naked in the stream
where you tried to conceal your sex
that's why I never call you by your new name, but only qanqon

from that moment on people refer to her as qanqon
this shames her and she keeps her jealous rages at bay
but now that her identity is out in the open
she's free just to be, and we begin to grow as women
the old ladies there spend many long hours with their teachings
and for a time we're happy

then as suddenly as the volcanic ash that marks our birth-time
her jealousy erupts when we're on a trip to kootenay lake
I warn her against mistreatment and she laughs a laugh
that could turn the blood cold in any person's veins
we take our quarrel into our canoe where, in view of everyone
she shoots an arrow into my wrist, a challenge, she says
to my professed spiritual protection
which has kept her from giving me the beating I so truly deserve

I'm calm, though broken-hearted, and I pull out the arrow
blood streaming down my arm and onto my clothes
I place the arrow on her lap and I begin to sing
rubbing my wrist and praying as my grandmother taught me
my wrist heals over immediately
I tell her then, qanqon kamek klaula, my love for you is unending
and though I know it'll be years before I'm myself again
the dream of us is ended here
tonight I pitch my lodge alone
tomorrow I return to my family

I'm from black bear white pine country
I'm known as petite muskwa, little bear
and I'm here to tell the final two parts of this story
in my youth I travel with my family to red river des métis
where my parents, ojibwe-cree-french métis
begin to harvest indian corn, potatoes and other garden foods
as well as the much-needed seneca root
sure remedy for snake bites, colds, croup, whooping cough
pneumonia and rheumatism
these my parents harvest in abundance
to provide for the numerous traders passing through

I grow into an ambitious young woman, restless and aware
for by now I speak seven languages well
cree, ojibwe, mohawk, mi'kmaw, wyandot, french, english
I'm trained by the old ones in the ways of mediation
and I'm skilled with a canoe, a bow and a gun
I travel often with the crews
on a good day I canoe a hundred miles, carrying a heavy load

in my travels, I learn of a woman further to the west
named qanqon kamek klaula, sitting-in-the-water-grizzly
who seeks a working companion to travel the fur trade trails
who will translate and mediate among the people
and guide the white man in those parts
for by now, in indian country it's a well-known fact
that the white man, whether french, english, irish, scot
are not democratic in their ways, and consensus is as foreign to them
as firewater is to us

so it is that greed among them is more common than kindness
and time after time the true meaning of sharing
is an outlandish notion, as horrifying
as when they witness a giveaway among our people
where often a family for reasons they themselves decide
even families who're rich with possessions and food
will give away all they have to others, only to start over with nothing
and in that way become the richest among us

while among the white man of our time
whether there's plenty to be had or very little
sharing what they have seldom enters their hearts or minds
except by small degree
and it's the observation of our elders
that unless by tough and gentle persuasions and teachings
from those among us inuit, indians and métis
who're gifted to communicate with the white man in this way
everywhere the white man dwells there will continue to be
those among them who grow fat and gather glitter
like crows at nesting time, while others literally starve to death
outside their timber fences and doors of polished wood

so it is I set out westward with my twin brother
and when we're close to our destination
at the tacousah tessah river, we're attacked by a grizzly
my brother dies there
and just as I give back his body to our mother earth
the man-like woman qanqon kamek klaula approaches from the south
and from that day forward, we work alongside one another as warriors
as couriers for white travellers and fur traders
as leaders of groups of traders, as healers of the sick

as we mature, we fast alone four days, four times each year
for seven years, and share our visions with the people along our travels
as we're instructed by our ancestors
and protectors from the spirit world

the white man believes we're a couple, man and wife
and though lovers, we're equals in terms of our knowledge
of men's and women's ways
I'm the smaller and finer boned
though we both dress in the beautiful clothing of my people
our leather tanned by our own hands and lovingly decorated
with intricate quillwork and embroidery

dressed in this way, on our first courier assignment together
we journey from a post on the spokan river
and in pursuit of other business
we follow the course of the tacousah tessah
which takes us deep into lands we're shown while fasting
we're to forewarn them that, after hundreds of thousands of years
of living on this land
there's a pending decimation of their peoples

following on the heels of the white fur traders
by means of a devastating plague they will call smallpox
and if that won't be enough, through the agency
of two enormous supernaturals who'll soon be on their way
one they'll call a gold rush, and one a train
who'll each in their turn overturn the very ground
only to bury lodges and villages underneath them

after weeks of leaving these messages of doom
and upon reaching the falls of the tacousah tessah
we learn from the coastal chinook people there
of white men at the mouth of the river
so in order to possibly cut our trip in half, we arrive at fort astoria
believing perhaps to find there
the man we're meant to meet at fort estekatakene
on what the white man calls the fraser river

instead, we're met with much fanfare
for our dress is unfamiliar in this region
and qanqon kamek klaula's language isn't known here
so although we both speak excellent english and french
we speak and are responded to in cree by a white man we befriend
and soon we're hired to guide his party to a place not far
from the spokan river
as we continue with our courier assignment

we tell the peoples along this way
of future times, some two hundred years from now
when a great outpouring of gifts will be made to them
by the white people and those others who come to this land
whose need for knowledge of the preservation
of earth, plant, water, air, four-legged, winged, salmon, mountain, sea
will become the primary need

these words are received with gratitude and gifts
and upon our arrival at oakinachen
we're accompanied by twenty-six horses
loaded with some of the most valuable articles
owned by the peoples along our way

all is well with us for eight years
despite a jealous streak in qanqon kamek klaula
that rivals anyone's, and is a mockery of our ways
so that when her moods are prone to rage
I spend those times in my own lodge built for this purpose
away from harm's way
one such morning I dream of a black bear
who's maimed by a grizzly

later that same day, I tell qanqon kamek klaula of this dream
and she tells me, yes, I'm done with you
you tell me to accept myself for who I am
to look into my centre of myself
and my constant bouts of rage will wane
like grandmother moon in her healing time

you tell me that anger's fear and fear's anger
have no place in the generations of our future
and you tell me to be warned about the dangers
of expanding our spiritual abilities
without a corresponding development of wisdom
all power corrupts you say, and spiritual power is no different

but I tell you, you're wrong and I don't have to agree with you
just because you believe you're right
must be the white in you my friend, for nothing can bring about change
better than good solid anger fuelled by exact fact

if you'd keep your mouth shut when I tell you to
and do as I say, keeping your thoughts to yourself
all would be well
this time I'm going home to my people with my share of our wealth
alone

I'm no longer known as petite muskwa
but as medicine bear woman
before I continue the fourth and final part of this story
I'll tell you this
we native women braid our hair for balance
of body, mind and spirit
a braid down the middle of your back can bring balance all day

these are my thoughts when I'm attacked by a grizzly
after recovering from a broken heart
when I lost qanqon kamek kluala
sitting-in-the-water-grizzly, to her rage

I'm injured badly, and I wear the marks today
with the right side of my face badly scarred
my right arm severed clean
when severely injured and barely holding on to breath
I plead with the great animal not to harm me further
and at this she turns and leaves

then I rise into the air and meet an old lady there
who tells me, petite muskwa, little bear
you must return to the lower kutenai
your work there is incomplete and you're to meet once again with
qanqon kamek klaula as your love and your companion
the two of you have many more years together
to bring peace and healing to young and old

the old lady then gives me a new name, medicine bear woman
she gives me a song to restore the dead to life
and the ability to cure many illnesses

the feast at the lake, which lasts many days
is where I meet qanqon kamek klaula once again
after five long years apart

my transformation is so complete
at first qanqon kamek klaula is frightened
by the very sight of me
she backs into a tree when she hears me speak
the beautiful voice of petite muskwa
reaching out from such a hideous face
but her fear lasts only a moment's breath
and after this we live many years together
in peace and haromony, kept busy with our healing work

for by now she's left those raging days behind
when she wouldn't hesitate to strike and beat another
she talks instead with grace and beauty
of how she's come to know herself
of how her blinded eyes and deafened ears
her own wounded heart, kept her from knowing herself
interfered like mud overtop of mud
with her healing gift, her gift of foreknowing

and, oh how she's changed
her talk is powerful and moving
and in her own words she asks how could she be
so filled with herself, with her own heartless rage
after only one life-altering year
with the white manservant
many years ago
then all the years of violence that followed

to throw a woman no bigger than a child
against a tree over and over and over again
to gratify her need to control even the thoughts and dreams
of another

and so it is one of the most beautiful women I know, inside and out
whose terrible sadness followed her around like an angry wind
has survived the terror, and is now like a song
long and tender, with laughter all around

no longer is she lonely with loss, so much loss forced on her
through brutal violence
but rather now, like never before
our love crawls inside our clothes, our eyes, our pores
communicates there in a wordless world
where commitments are solidified for a lifetime

ours is a bond blessed by the ancient ones
familiar touches, the way the touches feel
the way the touches promise, our secrets
I know love on this earth
doesn't get better than this
and if it did, chaos would occur

now here I'm going to describe
not our many years of work and peace
but the final mission of qanqon kamek klaula
which occurs when we're mature women
while we're called as peace messengers
to mediate at qomakne, on the horse plains
between the salish, who've become our family
and the blackfoot

qanqon kamek klaula, being the only one among us
who's permitted to travel freely among the camps
learns of a blackfoot plot to continue with the negotiations
as if for a peaceful resolution
and just when each party is relaxed and ready
to declare their agreement
the blackfoot will ambush the salish

the day is clear in my mind's eye still
I can feel the warm from the early summer sun
and the storm that moves in from the south
at the close of that most horrible of days
a day that to this day feels dreamlike and unreal

at sunrise we offer our thanks to the ancient ones
for this new day
qanqon kamek klaula is edgy and we take our time
while we discuss the day's negotiations which will take her
to the blackfoot camp
I tell her, no, don't go
today is a day of doom

she tells me, no my medicine bear woman
today is a day when we must face our fears
one small moment at a time
by nightfall we're expected to have a resolution and tomorrow a feast
and only the ancestors know what'll come between

so it is that not long after qanqon kamek klaula's departure
I hear battle cries from the blackfoot camp, each signalling the death
of a kutenai warrior
this conflict continues at breakneck speed and in a moment
my heart freezes to my bones

for I hear the voice of qanqon kamek klaula
powerful enough even to silence the birds and animals
and become one with the early afternoon sun

I run towards the blackfoot camp
but already they've moved further to the east and south
for they've started to make their way homeward
and her cries, her songs, seeming to last for an eternity
tell me she's faced with many and fighting for her life

finally, and long before I reach the site
a cry from a blackfoot warrior indicates her death
I wait where I am, crouched and concealed for an eternity
while the blackfoot prepare to leave

by now I'm aware the salish have moved camp
and I know the reason for qanqon kamek klaula's care with me
in the night
the lingering nature of our farewells earlier this dreaded day
for she, like I, knew that today was her day
to be greeted by her ancestors
her death voluntary, to save the salish party
who've made their way toward fort hall

I wait, and at last the blackfoot men
start to go, and pass along below me
and though there are many of them
only one or two sing their victory song
I wait many hours more before I leave my hiding place
and by now the only remaining kutenai warrior has joined me
we walk some distance along the side of the hill
before he descends to the trail to take home this dreadful news
and bring back others to help

night comes and even then, wary of the blackfoot
I don't start to give the mourning cry until close to dawn
when I go to where she is, propped against a pole
and there I wait with her until her family arrives

for two days, while the blackfoot make their way homeward
the two warriors primarily responsible for her death
very good friends with each other
are suddenly at each other's throats
and need to be separated several times
their leader approaches the two and tells them, men
you must realize that this woman's spirit continues to trouble us
we've killed a powerful woman, a strong woman and a great prophet
you're to continue the journey home while I go back with these others
to return this part of her heart to her people for a proper ceremony

and this he does
he arrives even before her family and he tells me
the purpose of his return
I tell him, go, they're on their way
and before his departure he tells me
it takes several shots to seriously wound qanqon kamek klaula
and while she's held in a seated position by several warriors
others slash her chest and abdomen with their knives

immediately afterwards the deep wounds heal themselves
and though this occurs several more times
she gives no more war cries

the blackfoot leader goes on to say, the last wound she's unable to heal
for one of the warriors slices open her chest to get at her heart
and cuts off the lower portion
which he's given to me here in this basket to return to her family

after qanqon kamek klaula's death
no wild animals or birds disturb her body
for even the animals and birds
recognize her spiritual gifts
and respect them

to prevent random shifts of subject in midstream
the eye of creation has an overbite

germaine:
her eyes see what the sky sees
a house full of birds

I've reached the fourth day of my fast. I'm back at the old medicine
woman's lodge, guarded by wolves. beside me is a wolf—quiet, still,
within arm's reach. with only a look, the wolf is able to shift what and
where I see. instantly, I'm inside the lodge. I know where I am as I slowly
realize that I've reached back and into my birth mother's past, to the
place of the origins of my métis ancestors several hundred years ago,
somewhere along the st. lawrence seaway and deep inside the great lakes.
once I'm inside, the old lady looks at me, full in the face, motions for me
to come sit next to her.

this time she speaks out loud, her voice rich, like rain on hot sand, and I
understand her as she explains in her ancient language, that this
is the fourth and final day of my fast. here, I will complete a cleansing
sweatlodge, after which I'll meet with a helper—the youngest michahai
yokuts two-spirit woman who didn't travel to pleiades of the sky world,
but rather who remained with mother earth and transformed to stone,
who will take me by the hand, and before I know what's up, what's
down, I'll wake up in my own bed.

the old lady tells me, what you've learned here will return home
with you and you're to share this knowledge as far and as wide as
your remaining years will allow you. without exception, the two-spirit
women who've shared with you on this journey are women whose
stories have been told and retold between the dusty old pages of
european missionaries and explorers, anthropologists and indian agents,
and again by modern european scholars.

these white people's perceptions, distorted by their fear, are not unlike a
rainbow circling the sun, warning of the heat that can destroy the fragile
birds in spring. they brought their armies, their diseases—then they
thought we'd all die off, my girl. but here we are still, and it's time for
you two-spirits to come forward and learn your roles once again. two-
spirit people are needed now. like these amazing ancestors from your
past, my girl, you two-spirits will be asked to be mindful of the coming
storms that will change the face of mother earth forever.

when you return home, at first you'll feel lonely for this place, the pace you've grown accustomed to. you'll find you need to spend a lot of time alone. follow those feelings—on the evening breeze, on the back of a monarch, inside the eyes of a dragonfly.

you've met so many women, their voices clear against this evening's grace, their music wrapped inside them. their feet moving rhythmically down a road that leads inside mother earth, where air transforms to sand and water and stone, and thought becomes rich with leaf. each woman you've met here—and the countless women whose stories haven't yet been told—lives inside each of us, my girl.

the wolf shifts my view once again, and there is shirley bear, her words a canvas, her small frame's shadow casting blues and reds and browns across the waters, intensified by the day's light. her silver hair blows like dew on stone, one small drop at a time. listen, now, says the old lady, to what shirley bear has to say about the fourth sacred direction that completes your circle of learning here.

shirley bear, maliseet woman
recites the northward path
her poem from *virgin bones:*
belayak kcikug'nas'ikn'ug
"the vocation of storytelling"

the north wind, with her frosty breath
unmercifully freezes
all that she comes in contact with

the most ingenious of creation
survives the relentless cold
her sister, the earth
rests from her long productive year
and the relations who are directed to
sleep with her

the white sister tells her story
listen

listen. remember where you come from, germaine, says the old lady. always remember, it's important to know what you can from your past. we are our past. forever remember sky woman. she's your first mother. and remember, when sky woman fell from the sky at the beginning times on this here turtle island she wasn't alone. first, loon and heron put together their great wings and stopped her free-fall. then, eagle saw them flying there, getting very tired under sky woman's great weight. eagle talked to grandfather turtle and suggested a council of the elders be held, where a great discussion took place. should we take her? should we save her? she'll drown if we don't. mother earth might be hurt by that.

and so went their discussion until that great snapping turtle offered his back so sky woman could live. others, like bass, offered herself as food. still others, the otter and the muskrat, sacrificed their lives while attempting to get mud from the bottom of the sea to provide earth for sky woman to live on turtle's back. beaver, too, offered to get the mud, and he was successful. tremendous co-operation and sacrifice prompted this great and permanent change on our mother earth, and grandfather turtle sacrificed his world as he knew it to be transformed into turtle island.

the old medicine woman grew silent. she and all the other women I'd met here gathered outside the sweatlodge to begin the ceremony. as I waited my turn to enter, I was reminded, this was the creation story I grew up hearing. sky woman was the first woman. she was the first mother and the first grandmother to my ancestors. sky woman's ways of knowing, her ways of thinking and doing, her ways of seeing, are all around us. as indigenous peoples, we're still here after more than two hundred fifty thousand years on this continent. the ways of our ancestors are still here.

167

I have so much to be thankful for, so many women to thank. they'll remain in my thoughts for the rest of my life. I'm an artist, and I realize I must begin a series of embroidered images where I'll stitch together what I've experienced here, bringing my ancestors to life again that way. theirs will be a sky whose blue hides behind a fine ribbon of hope, a glow that grows outward from sundogs reaching for the horizon of mother earth, violet-red-yellow-two-tone-blue. these are my thoughts as I enter the sweatlodge.

after the sweatlodge
the youngest michahai yokuts two-spirit woman
who doesn't travel to pleiades of the sky world
but rather who remains with mother earth
and transforms to stone
her face ochre
her mouth like fire
before she takes me home
holds a small bag of sacred sage
women's medicine
takes the sage around every circle of women
of all nations, all our relations
yellow, red, black, white
who gather together for whatever sacred reason

invites each woman to take some sage
to form a small ball with the sage in her hands
to rub herself where she needs healing
to ask the spirit of that sage
to take away her fears
to purify her

as the women do this
they pray each in her own way
and as they start to put back the sage
into the small bag
the bag fills with light and glorious song

we are sisters on a journey, singing in the sun
singing through the darkest night
the healing has begun, begun
the healing has begun

we are sisters on a journey, singing now as one
remenbering the ancient ones
the women and their wisdom
the women and their wisdom

young crow:
the parts of the eyes that are tender
wrens hiding under snow

crows lined up on telephone wire
seeming sweet and resting-like
but ready to swarm
crows will gather round
another crow
and berate that crow
for a severe wrongdoing
kill the crow or crows
or leave them there to die

crows on high-rises, returning from winter flight. birds at play, their tail
feathers spread like simple lines across a long and lovely day. birds of
prey, a play on words. this is me, young crow talking. how can you tell
I watched several violent movies on the weekend? one where everyone
ends up dead in the desert.

just when I'm waking up from a kak-nap, I'm thinking it'd be nice if life
was a word processing package and all fundamental errors in thought
and deed were automatically corrected. and right now? I feel like a hole
between my thoughts. looking for answers? sing along with the music
inside my head. sounds like a high-rise full of birds, clouding over in
each others' rooms, colourful and long, all talking all at once, feeling
right at home. no furniture upstairs? just a bunch of old violet-red-
yellow-two-tone-blueflies, all having the same dream down under an
overpass, bridges that house the birds.

lesson for the day's end? crow is not an omen of death or whatever it
is. we like to eat dead things, that's all. somebody has to. just cuz we
don't cook them doesn't make us evil. crow's a shapeshifter and brings
messages for the future. maw-caws say the ancient ones make no one
evil, that evil's up to the individual. we pick and we choose. sure hope
that's true. I can almost sense a narrative playing its way out of this
story, and along comes old maw-caw to brighten up my evening. I can't
find the fleshly woman again, see? and I'm worried. it's right around

day's end and the moon is rising, and, well? I'm worried. it's the fleshly
woman's fourth and final day and I'm starting to panic. when I panic,
I get all caught up in my own head-kak. maw-caw tells me I ought to
wear a helmet, like a skateboarder, 'cept for brain-blogs.

so maw-caw tells me a story to calm me down. could of parked two
cars in my mouth while she's telling me this one, my mouth opens itself
so wide. basically, what she tells me in ten words or less is, I'm dead. I
mean, since I can remember, I've straddled the worlds—mostly just to
get away or for vacation—but dead?

so I've been talking up a resting horse's arse all along? I'm just a poetic
device? maw-caw laughs, says, yeah, me too. small spotted eagle, too.
death is the gateway to a new life, young crow, and the fleshly woman
has gone back to the world of the living. small spotted eage is watching
over her over there right now. you can go too, eh?

maw-caw continues. you and me, like any crow, bring important
messages to the living, messages of the straight-shooting kind crows
are famous for. we're well-known for our parenting skills, too, and for
having close-knit families and friends. us crows are magic, see? and
that's why us three, you, me and the small spotted eagle? that's why
we've been brought together here, says maw-caw.

you, because you and your ego were brought back to life by the fleshly
woman when she was still a girl and you were just a chick-kak. small
spotted eagle because she holds the history for the two-spirit women.
and me? because of our centuries with the métis. us crows and them
métis? we've stuck together like fly poop to a blanket ever since any
maw-caw can remember. like with us crows with our attractive, dainty,
agile, fast, little feet, the métis have their sash. those métis wear that sash
on special occasions and anytime they like cuz the intricate braid-like
weaving on that sash symbolizes togetherness, looking after each other,
maintaining a nation and caring for one another.

I was truly moved. and confused. ego? I say to maw-caw, doesn't that have something to do with popcorn? or i.d. papers? birth cirtificates, métis cards, scrip, that sort of fluffy-puffy-stuff? not one of my favourites, popcorn. gets caught inside my beak. can't talk. and just when I think I've heard it all.

keep talking, I say to myself. don't stop. okay, all the stuff that happened over the last few days is like a daniel david moses play, then? like tomson highway or marie clements, alice lee or even shakespeare? happened real fast. good thing there were no tragedies far as I'm concerned. that is, if you don't count the fact that I died somewheres over the past several years and I didn't even remember. here I've been scared of death all my life. and death. just goes to show you.

am I preaching? am I? for those of you who don't know, the rainbow colours—violet-red-yellow-two-tone-blue—represent the pride colours. you know? lesbian and gay folk? transgendered? transexual? bisexual? the many genders of the olden days on this here turtle island. things've finally started to change since cartier slipped into the st. lawrence looking for gold. heck, in canada, the two-spirits can get married all legal-like now. just a few years back, by law, they were considered bonafidely crazy. truth is, those old ones who created us all? they don't make mistakes. it's all about balance. plain and simple.

well, I'll be signing off now before the noise in my head gets to youse. besides, now that I know I'm dead? I'm ready to test out my acting skills. maybe compose a few dirges. first, though, I'll fly to the other side to find small spotted eagle and have a look-see how that fleshly woman's homecoming's coming along. high five!

caw

caw

caw

caw

gopher (with one eff):
geese inside her eyes
intelligent and kind

letter to germaine:

yesterday was a day full of shadows, even and long, like walking at the
end of a long summer day. there's so much more going on than
a lifetime could say, and, try as i may, the less is more than i expected.
me being me, i need more time to process, to distance myself from my
own fractured self, a mathematical puzzle where the numbers are words,
and a sentence, key to the logic of the story, has found her way home
and left everyone else behind.

oh dear, i'm starting to sound like a crow. must be the snow. this
morning, i wake myself up laughing. in that instant, my cell phone
rings. it's aptn again, reminding me i have an interview today on their
show—in the company of two-spirit women, the show's called. chinook
depending, i was scheduled to appear on today's show with you, and,
as it happens, i'm thankful there's an early spring chinook because
otherwise i'd be a no-go.

despite the fact that you've been gone for months now, i feel vibrant
and very alive while walking through downtown. the beauty of this
place, this land, can be felt even here, in the heart of the city, through
the cement and the high-rises. my home my tumble try.

there's been a shift in the weather that's magnified by the cold, and now
there's thunder in the air. it's a time of great change, and today, in the ice
and snow—the bitter-sweet warmth and very bad roads—i cross town
to learn what i didn't know i already knew. i'm late, so i enter the studio
from the side door. i can see the back of my empty chair, and i can see
the chair beside mine, filled with none other than you-know-who!

i listen to your rhythmic, familiar voice, a voice like summer rain, and i
know you can see now—even with closed eyes—you can see through to
the unseen and perceive things and coming events that are hidden from
others. you can look into the future, and into the secrets of our dreams.

now i wait
for the end of the honey
empty jar and new moon's
full blossomed sheets
a thousand years
of healing

so happy you're home,
gopher (with one eff)

small spotted eagle:
the eyes of a small snowy owl
walking into ceremony

bird sanctuaries are serious and lovely places, and the birds, ever so grateful, take advantage of this small human kindness. these are her thoughts as small spotted eagle takes her final moments in the world of the visibles, the young crow on her back, surrounded by bird people from all over who're stopping to rest or who're just beginning to return from their winter homes. she's been here a while now, watching over the fleshly woman's homecoming, and she's been waiting to see the little gopher's response when she's reunited with her dear friend.

at the end of her fourth day of her fast, the fleshly woman stepped out of the sweatlodge and walked in the direction of the sun. she walked all the way back to the moment of the youngest michahai yokuts two-spirit woman, and at their coming togther, the youngest michahai yokuts two-spirit woman—her grace, her smell, her breath, ancient—took the fleshly woman by the hand. she told the fleshly woman, upon her return to her homeland, she's to take a new spirit name, and that name is cleansing rain woman. come, she said, and I'll take you to where there's a painting on the north door.

and in that instant, they were there, where they saw a painting of a beautiful woman, wind, a tree—their reflections in each others' sounds. the fleshly woman knew her whole life was there, in one single curve of the paintbrush, her present, her past and her future. with that thought, she became the cottonwood in the painting, and she knew what it was to be completely exposed to the world, nothing hidden or held back.

she felt like she could see everything and everyone she'd ever meet in her lifetime, her heart open. her emotions—raw, broken—were profound, and the fleshly woman knew she was meant to understand something with her heart, a song she knew already.

small spotted eagle was reminded of details of ancient cave and rock drawings, where all the exaggerated parts fall away from themselves and expose, not the brain of a human or an animal, but a stomach or a liver or a heart. head-knowing can't be trusted and that's why there are no brains depicted next to the hearts and other organs in the ancient drawings.

the heart-knowing we can trust. the heart is the home, the safety, the place where emotion has the answers to any and all the hard questions. the answers are all inside.

so it is here, from the heart of the great cottonwood, that the fleshly woman hears the hushed tones of many women swirling around her, inside her, like the rippling growth rings, the cottonwood's internal medicine wheel. only when the women's voices give way to the smooth, sweet sap inside the tree will the fleshly woman once again take the hand of the youngest michahai yokuts two-spirit woman, who will guide her back and through the violet-red-yellow-two-tone-blue mists of a rainbow, to wake up in her own bed.

the fleshly woman's heart and head are living in each other's rooms now, aware of the other's presence. her heart needs time to communicate to her head the level of work, the time that's needed, even on a busy day, to take the time it takes. change the past to change the storm is what she's left holding on to. always, behind the storm, ahead of the storm, on the other side of the storm, there is sun. even with this knowing, a storm is a storm, a necessary event that brings about renewal and new life here on mother earth.

the fleshly woman is returned to her home knowing the gifts of the two-spirits, and, ever so slowly, she'll begin to understand her role, a crucial role in opening the doors that resist opening. for her convenience, young crow takes out his mechanical pencil and composes a five-verse poem, pinning the verses—one in each doorway and one in the centre—for the

fleshly woman to find. he titles the five-verse poem, four on the door, or,
infant laughter rises, fills the dawn.

loving women is like a gentle touch on a wrist
sore from a day of cutting wood
on the back of a hand, writing on the computer
on every word that's uttered
from sweet full lips
two-spirit people are not a typo
but are here for good, for all time
to ensure balance in body, mind, heart, spirit

soon
each woman who loves
another woman
and is forced to bury her glee
behind a mask of fear
will open her arms to herself
and her people will open their arms
to her

all over turtle island
the welcome will be genuine
as countless two-spirit women
negotiate disputes
with tremendous results
even the spider and especially the gopher
will help her to achieve this goal

there are hundreds of thousands
of two-spirit women
some nations boast two or three
for every ten people
this generation
there're reasons

our services are needed
now
in our time
healing and opening doors
violet-red-yellow-two-tone-blue
doors long closed

in indigenous cultures, we don't do things alone. the two-spirit women
in our communities—in the villages, towns and cities—will open those
doors and out will come the most amazing stories, reaching beyond the
snowy-topped mountains. we don't have a lead voice. there are brave
two-spirit women from each generation to give life to their stories. and
so it begins.

small spotted eagle and young crow see the fleshly woman for the
last time now. it's about a month since her fourth and final day in
small spotted eagle's homeworld, when the fleshly woman travelled
to the st. lawrence seaway, the great lakes—the birthplace of her métis
ancestors. those mountains and waters contain more knowledge than
anyone could endure. like a smudge, the air is sacred and generous with
wisdom. as small spotted eagle and young crow prepare to return home,
they hear the voice of mother earth on the northwind, a whisper that
swells into song.

live your life to the fullest
breathe in our light
our greens
our ochre scent
listen for the wind
and play with your loves of your life
sing, my children, sing

moma I can feel you under my feet
moma I can feel your heart beat
moma I can feel you under my feet
moma I can feel your heart beat

hey-ya-hey-ya-hey-ya-hey-ya-hey-ya-hey-ya-ho
hey-ya-hey-ya-hey-ya-hey-ya-hey-ho-ho-oh-ho
hey-ya-hey-ya-hey-ya-hey-ya-hey-ya-hey-ya-ho
hey-ya-hey-ya-hey-ya-hey-ya-hey-ho-ho-oh-ho

mother earth:
loon spirit lingers
and the mountains are saving us from ourselves

I am earth mother   with care and grace I nurture
          my children   darkness and light   death and
renewal   trust   as the seed of the newly formed   I am all
that you need and I give all that I am   and yet
                    so much destruction in so short a time
          ask the cockroach ask the loon   the ancient bones of your
ancestors   digging for gold   oil bleeds the land
          earthquake

I am earth mother
always remember blood
the giver of life
can be manipulated
by medicine ways

like fire from a candle
a sacred fire
fire is life's blood

in my womb there is fire
a love so deep
too deep for comprehension
for words or breath

is life's tender   remember   all stones in your path
          are alive   they are my backbone   given
               by the grandmothers and grandfathers

if you can truly trust your earth mother   as the plants do
          a note pinned onto a door   the richest plan
               is not to have one

ACKNOWLEDGMENTS

First and foremost, I would like to thank the mysteries, the grandmothers and grandfathers, for each new day, for the gift of story. To the Keepers of the stories, meegwich.

In memory of Paula Gunn Allen, for being a grandmother of the light, an inspiration for the seven generations who follow.

To Shirley Bear, for your wisdom and grace, for generously allowing me to cocoon this story within the circle of your poem, "The Vocation of Storytelling," from *Virgin Bones: Belayak Kcikug'nas'ikn'ug*, and for your twin dreaming of my title thirty years before me.

To my children, Graham and Barb, and to my son-in-law, Harold, for your constant encouragement and love. My grandchildren, Willow, Jessinia and Mazie, may your lives be filled with story and song. To Adrian, for staying close. Always, my sister, Joy.

To my good friends Margie Faccini-Lee and Carla Osborne, for reading earlier drafts, and Clô Laurencelle for your beautiful cover art.

This book was eleven years in the making. Without the ancestors, those women who smoothed the ground and had the foresight to present their stories to European men for publication, this story would not be possible. Thank you for providing a chronicle of the past in order to build a future and a rebirthing of our traditional roles and names in the present—geenumu gesallagee, agokwa, okitcitakwe, ake:skassi—only a thimble-full of our namings of ourselves in our mother tongues before contact. I consulted with Elders at length during the making of this book, and I was advised to retell the mainstream published versions in the first person, in order to reclaim these two-spirit women's stories. I therefore apologize to the Keepers for any errors in the tellings.

To Renée Lang for generously offering the quiet of your home and garden to complete the final draft, and to the fine gang of artists at Parkdale's Mezzrow's. Youse rock!

Grants were generously provided by the Canada Council for the Arts —Aboriginal Arts, and the Alberta Foundation for the Arts.

Adaptations of the crow character—"Young Crow-Caw Caught in Calgary," and "Young Crow-Caw Loses an Eyeball"—appear in *Tales From Mocassin Avenue* (2006), and an early draft of the chapter, "on the other side are the correlatives for a balanced life: education, process & ceremony," was published in *portfolio milieu 2004*.

The term "two-spirit" is the english translation of the Anishinaubae, niizh manitoag, coined at a gathering of lesbian, gay, bisexual, transgendered, transsexual Native peoples in Winnipeg, Canada, in 1990. I respectfully acknowledge that there are many who do not identify with what has now become a pan-Native descriptor.

Allen, Paula Gunn. 1991. *Grandmothers of the Light: A Medicine Woman's Sourcebook*. Boston: Beacon Press.

_____. 1986. *The Sacred Hoop: Recovering the Feminine in American Indian Traditions*. Boston: Beacon Press.

Bear, Shirley. 2006. *Virgin Bones: Belayak Keikug'nas'ikn'ug*. Toronto: McGilligan Books.

Brant, Beth, Ed. 1988. *A Gathering of Spirit: Anthology of North American Indian Women*. Ithaca, New York: Firebrand Books.

Jacobs, Sue-Ellen, Wesley Thomas, Sabine Lang, Eds. 1997. *Two-Spirit People: Native American Gender Identity, Sexuality, and Spirituality*. Chicago: University of Illinois Press.

Lang, Sabine. 1998. *Men as Women, Women as Men: Changing Gender in Native American Culture*. Austin: University of Texas Press.

Proulx-Turner, Sharron. 2008. "she walks for days/ inside a thousand eyes/ a two-spirit story." *Spirit Magazine*, Vol. 4, Issue 4, pp.15-16.

Rosco, Will. 1998. *Changing Ones: Third and Fourth Genders in Native North America*. New York: St. Martin's Griffin.

_____. 1988. *Living the Spirit: A Gay American Indian Anthology*. New York: St. Martin's Press.

Williams, Walter L. 1986. *The Spirit and the Flesh: Sexual Diversity in American Indian Culture*. Boston: Beacon Press.